Piecemeal

30 Bold Ingredients ➕ 90 Variations

Piecemeal

A Meal-Planning Repertoire with 120 Recipes
to Make in 5+, 15+, or 30+ Minutes

Kathryn Pauline

CHRONICLE BOOKS

SAN FRANCISCO

For Romy and Peter, who moved a far piece from
home so we could live with authenticity and joy.

Library of Congress Cataloging-
in-Publication Data available.

ISBN 978-1-7972-1986-8

Manufactured in China.

MIX
Paper from
responsible sources
FSC™ C169962

Photography by Kathryn Pauline.
Prop and food styling by Kathryn Pauline.
Design by Margherita Buzzi.

10 9 8 7 6 5 4 3 2 1

Chronicle books and gifts are available at
special quantity discounts to corporations,
professional associations, literacy
programs, and other organizations. For
details and discount information, please
contact our premiums department at
corporatesales@chroniclebooks.com
or at 1-800-759-0190.

Chronicle Books LLC
680 Second Street
San Francisco, California 94107
www.chroniclebooks.com

Contents

Fruits, compotes, and curds

Recipe list

This book's table of contents is ordered around 30 super-flavorful components. But for easy browsing, we've also included a list that's organized by category:

Spinach salad	238
Steak salad with salsa verde	168
Tabbouleh	72
Well-red chopped salad	34

Mains

Beet Reubens	32
Bibimbap	186
Bún	132
Butter-basted lamb chops with pickled mango	228
Cauliflower burritos	42
Cheesy meatball bake with spinach	120
Chicago-style deep-dish pizza	58
Coconut shrimp tacos with cabbage slaw	114
Cold soba noodles	194
Cornmeal pancake stack	106
Falafel crumble pita pocket	232
Garlicky PLTs	176
Gochujang meatloaf	184
Grilled steak with jammy onion chutney	86
Katsu curry with coconut shrimp	116
Larb gai	74
Masgouf	230
Meatballs with mashed potatoes and gravy	124
Mujadara	90
Pizza bianca ai funghi	82
Pork chops with nectarine salsa	254
Spaghetti aglio e olio	66
Sweet potato broccoli grain bowls	96
Toum thyme chicken	178
Tzatziki fried chicken	204
Za'atar chickpeas with yellow rice	202

Sweets

Apple cream puffs with cinnamon craquelin	214
Black Forest mousse	260
Cherry almond cheese babka	264
Cherry chèvre cheesecake	262
Chocolate rugelach	274
Cream scones with passion fruit curd	278
Frozen milk chocolate passion fruit bars	282
Lemon grape poppy cake	224
Miso sweet potato caramel brownies	98
Mulled wine pears with mascarpone and streusel	244
Passion fruit olive oil cake	280
Polish plum cake	256
Puff pastry tartlets	246
Spiced chocolate pear cake	248
Strawberry rhubarb fool	270
Strawberry shortcakes	252
Vegan double-chocolate orange tart	240
Victoria sponge cake	272
Warm apples with Thai tea ice cream	212

Introduction

All of my friends lived within a 10-minute walk of my apartment throughout my twenties. My husband and I would leave the windows open all summer long, and every once in a while, we'd hear Erin's voice and see the top of Alvin's hat peeking out above the sill.

Erin and Alvin never showed up empty-handed: They brought hot pepper jelly, caramelized tomatoes, a giant bunch of herbs, salsa roja—the list goes on. We'd hang out and come up with ways to put these components to good use.

Let's buy a sheet of cornbread and top it with goat cheese and caramelized tomatoes. Let's throw together a quick tabbouleh. Let's procrastinate and make tamales!

Erin and Alvin have life figured out. Their philosophy: When you amass a trove of flavorful bits and pieces, dinner cooks itself.

Piecemeal embraces this philosophy. This book will teach you how to make a variety of magical components, stash them away, and use them throughout the week to add a spark of excitement to every dish you prepare.

Here I've gathered my 30 favorite flavor-packed components. These puzzle pieces are not just useful—they are transformative. They breathe life into simple foundations such as pizza dough, lettuce, and chicken breast.

Each super-flavorful component comes with three recipes that feature it (taking a minimum of 5, 15, and 30 minutes), and includes instructions for storage, plus riffy ideas for using it.

It's your choice: Follow a recipe or wing it. Take your time or make something spur of the moment. Stick to a plan or switch gears. Use this book to do whatever works best for you.

How to use this book

This book is organized around 30 super-flavorful components: sauces, proteins, veggies, and more. Each of these base recipes is followed by 3 recipes that feature it. You'll also find a treasure trove of handy tips, ideas for improvising, and inspiration far beyond the recipes in this book. Here's a quick example that illustrates the concept of the cookbook:

1 batch recipe = 3 meals

Make a batch of smoky eggplant and store it in the fridge or freezer. Use the smoky eggplant in any of its 3 accompanying recipes:

5+ minute recipe: Make baba ganoush with just a few simple pantry ingredients and 5 minutes of extra active time. (Perfect for those times when you want to get something delicious on the table without much ado.)

15+ minute recipe: Buy a few more fresh ingredients to make a ricotta frittata with eggplant, chives, and tomato.

30+ minute recipe: Make a Chicago-style deep-dish pizza with eggplant and basil. (A little bit more of a weekend project, but you're already halfway there with smoky eggplant stashed away in the fridge.)

Improvisational ideas: Do your own thing! You'll find lots of ideas following each component, so let your inspiration run wild, guided by what ingredients you have on hand, or what you feel like eating. For example:

— Adapt the bruschetta on page 48 to feature smoky eggplant.
— Layer a few strips of eggplant into your favorite lasagna recipe.
— Save the smoky eggplant for another time, and make that deep-dish pizza with the garlicky mushrooms on page 77 instead.

These are the qualities that make each of these 30 components magical:

Bold: Components do all the heavy lifting. Each component adds that special flavor or texture that makes a recipe your favorite.

Storable: Components can be made ahead and stored without loss of quality. Most can be frozen for at least 3 months. Ones that can't be frozen will keep for at least several days in the fridge.

Versatile: The component has possibilities beyond its 3 accompanying recipes, with ways to use it in other recipes in this book and elsewhere.

Efficient: Component prep shouldn't add redundant or unnecessary cooking steps. The time you spend building flavor into the component will directly translate into future recipes; it's time well spent that your future self will thank you for.

How to use this book to improvise

This book encourages creativity and flexibility. So while you can just cook your way through it conventionally, here are a few prompts for improvisation:

3 ways to start with a component:
— Make a component, then wait to decide which of its 3 accompanying recipes you want to use it in. Maybe you end up having an unusually busy week, with time only to make the easiest recipe. Or maybe you feel inspired to make all 3. Either way, you've built flexibility into your meal prep schedule.

— Look through your component's list of other recipes from this book that you can adapt to feature it. Don't feel limited to the 3 accompanying recipes.
— Find inspiration by skimming the list of more things to try with your component. You'll find lots more ideas, so don't feel limited to the recipes in this book. For example, you can layer the smoky eggplant into your favorite vegetable lasagna recipe.

2 ways to start with a recipe:
— Try one of the 5 Easy Backup Plans on page 22, which go with most components in this book. When all else fails, make some avocado toast and call it a day!
— Skim through the recipes in the book, and check out their substitutions lists to shake things up. For instance, if you want to make the grain bowls on page 96, you'll find a list of 8 other components you can use to change up the flavor profile.

4 ways to go beyond this book:
— Make a list of your favorite dishes to cook or bake. Skim through the components in this book, find one that would go well with one of your favorites, and then try working the component in.
— Make a bunch of components, stash them away, and literally never even bother looking at a single recipe in this book. Use them however and whenever you feel inspired to.
— Look at the list of essential foundations on page 20, and think of some new ways you might combine them with some of this book's flavorful components to create something completely new.
— Make a list of some of your favorite super-flavorful components that aren't in this book, and think about how you might incorporate them into some of this book's recipes. They don't all have to be homemade items—good store-bought dressings, chutneys, and compotes all work great. Think of that sauce you put on absolutely everything or your favorite salad dressing. Or think back to recipes you've made in the past, and try to find bits and pieces to borrow and adapt—for instance, a honey mustard dressing that's part of your favorite grain bowl recipe might make a delicious salad dressing. See page 13 for a list of qualities that make a great component, so you'll always know what to keep an eye out for.

Why I cook with components

Meal-prepping routines work great for the hyper-organized, but most of us don't have the time or bandwidth to implement those methods in our lives. A handful of virtuosos on the other side of the spectrum can whip up an incredible dinner with zero planning and an almost-empty fridge. But most of us crave more support and structure, and this book is for you, because it will show you how to:

Work piecemeal, instead of all at once.
Instead of cooking a giant meal and reheating throughout the week, do a little work ahead of time, and then assemble or finish cooking "a la minute" for fresher meals that reflect, on a daily basis, what you feel like eating.

Meal plan with built-in flexibility.
These components store well, so you can approach the meal you envisioned with minimal commitment, while nothing goes to waste. If you end up having a busy week, you have easy backup plans to use up or store the component you prepped.

Cook only when you feel inspired to.
Prep a few components one weekend, store them, and cook your way through them when you feel like it.

Make small batches or giant batches.
Typical small-batch cooking is a pain, since it produces less food for the same amount of effort. But it's super efficient to make a big batch of a component and use it a few different ways throughout the week (or store freezable components, and use them over months).

A note on storage

The components in this book keep for at least a few days—and often for much longer—when frozen or refrigerated. Since I am by no means a homesteader (and odds are, neither are you), for me, long-term "preserving" does not involve boiling jars and pressure cooking to fix a seal. My version of preservation involves a freezer and five simple guidelines.

If you've been using your freezer as a dumping ground for questionable leftovers, your idea of how to use it is going to take some reframing. Instead, think of your freezer as a miraculous piece of technology that stops time in its tracks. Just follow these principles to get your freezer to work for you:

Learn to love your freezer: With certain items, freezing will result in absolutely no loss of quality. Freezing actually preserves quality better in many cases. Don't think of freezing as a last resort. In this book, if I note that a component freezes particularly well, this means that freezing it properly will extend its life and it will maintain good flavor and texture.

Freeze early: When you've finished preparing a food that freezes well, don't stick it in the fridge to languish, and then decide to freeze it five days later. Pop it straight into the freezer while it's still fresh, and then use it on your own time (even if that happens to be the very next day). For a component that's best enjoyed fresh, but can be frozen with little loss of quality, freeze on day two to give yourself a chance to enjoy it fresh, while doing your best to prevent the freezer from becoming a graveyard.

Freeze with thawing in mind: Don't freeze food in a way that will make it difficult to thaw later. Portion before freezing; freeze in single or double servings, or in small quantities if you're freezing pesto or other sauces that can be added to dishes. Take advantage of small containers and ice cube trays. Arrange loose items, such as slow-roasted tomatoes or roasted grapes, on a parchment-lined sheet pan, freeze until solid, then transfer to a tightly sealed plastic bag.

Get rid of air: The more air you can squeeze out of the bag/container and the tighter the seal, the longer you can freeze things without loss of quality. Liquids in tightly sealed containers as well as items in vacuum-sealed bags will last in the freezer for around 6 months (often longer). If you're freezing loose items in a resealable plastic bag, you're looking at more like 3 months or so. (Just don't vacuum-seal for the fridge or pantry unless you know what you're doing, as certain items carry a botulism risk.)

Label it: Since I will not remember what that mysterious bag of gray stuff is 2 months from now (and neither will you), labeling it with the item name and date makes life easier. Just make sure your labeling gear is convenient and inexpensive—a Sharpie, masking tape, and whatever freezer-safe containers you've got will work great, as long as it's all in an easy-to-access spot (buy a few extra Sharpies for when your family or housemates steal the pen from the kitchen). In a freezer full of labeled things, you'll be able to quickly see what you've got, and your freezer will become a source of inspiration instead of a guilty reminder of food waste.

Commonly used produce sizes

When the fruit and vegetables in this book are listed in the ingredient list without a size description or weight (for instance, simply as "2 tomatoes"), you can assume I mean a medium-size piece of fruit or vegetable (in other words, "2 medium tomatoes").

I'm putting this chart here as a reference, because even though this was my guide in developing these recipes, you, reader, will use what you have or can buy. And that's not always "medium tomatoes," right? Sometimes the best-looking tomatoes are the tiny grape-size ones; sometimes the market is musky with giant late-summer heirlooms. Use this chart to help you have a general sense of how much to use.

Feel free to eyeball it—if your tomatoes are large, use fewer, and if they are small, use more. For anyone with a digital scale and an obsession with precision, here are my exact weighed amounts. I test all my recipes by weighing everything, even liquids, in grams, so you can count on these numbers corresponding to the recipes in this book.

1 medium bell pepper	140 g	5 oz
1 medium butternut squash	1 kg	2¼ lb
1 head cauliflower	800 g	1¾ lb
1 large head cauliflower	1100 g	2½ lb
1 medium carrot	70 g	2½ oz
1 large bunch cilantro, leaves and tender stems	80 g	3 oz
1 English cucumber	400 g	14 oz
1 Persian cucumber	100 g	3½ oz
1 green onion	20 g	¾ oz
1 medium onion	180 g	6½ oz
1 large onion	240 g	8½ oz
1 medium orange	150 g	5¼ oz
1 large orange	250 g	8¾ oz
1 medium head radicchio	225 g	8 oz
1 small head radicchio	115 g	4 oz
1 medium russet potato	220 g	8 oz
1 medium sweet potato	180 g	6½ oz
1 medium tomato	150 g	5¼ oz
1 medium zucchini	200 g	7 oz

Essential foundations

The meals you make with the 30 components featured in this book are centerpieces. Each is a gorgeous floral arrangement that draws the eye, adds excitement to the table, and serves as a point of conversation. The components are the big, bold blooms at the center of the arrangements.

Slightly less exciting but no less important are essential foundations. These are the elements that anchor the components and help them exhibit their charisma. Think: a good vase, a flower frog, the wires, the leafy stems, and the branches that aren't the showstoppers, but hold those gorgeous, nodding peonies aloft.

Essential foundations are the chicken breast, pizza dough, and poached eggs—not the most exciting items, but the bases to carry flavorful components like the ones in this book.

I've put together a list of a few of my favorite essential foundations. Each one is easy to lift right out of a recipe and use as you wish, and some are so simple they don't even require instruction. Think about using them to help you incorporate exciting flavors and provide contrasting textures in the meals you cook.

5 easy backup plans

Consider these 5 easy dishes as the universal recipients of any topping, sauce, sauté, or drizzle in this book. In other words: Put your components on these when you don't feel like cooking or coming up with any other ideas for using them. At least one of these dishes will work.

Avocado toast is a true champion, since it's compatible with most of the components in this book. A frozen pizza or ricotta frittata each works great for using up most vegetable or meat components. A cheese board works great with most meats, vegetables, fruits, and a few of the sauces in this book. And if you're looking to use up something sweet, look no further than a classic English fool.

Avocado toast
Toss ripe avocado slices with some lime juice, salt, garlic powder, and black pepper. Toast some bread, then smash the avocado onto the bread with a fork. Top with a component or two, and enjoy. You can also add one or two additional flavorful ingredients, if they complement the component (for instance, feta, chèvre, sliced green onions, or sesame seeds).

While almost all of the components from this book are very happy atop avocado toast, stay away from meatballs, cinnamon apples, mulled wine pears, passion fruit curd, cherry compote, or strawberry rhubarb compote. If you're using a sauce or dressing from this book, consider adding a little produce; for example, arugula or sliced radishes go with most sauces.

Upgraded frozen pizza

Buy a frozen cheese pizza, top sparingly with something super flavorful, bake, and enjoy. Be careful not to overload your pizza with extra toppings (lest it get soggy or heavy), and add just enough for a little extra flavor.

Most of the meat and vegetable components work with this one and give you plenty of options, so stay away from the fruit components and the sauces/dressings. Also stay away from miso sweet potatoes, which are tricky to pair with cheese and tomato sauce. If you're using leafy herbs, add them after the pizza comes out of the oven (stay away from mint, which is another tricky one to pair). If you're using meatballs, cut them in half before placing them on top to prevent runaways.

Ricotta frittata

See page 56 for cooking instructions, and use any component you might use on a pizza (see above).

Cheese board

Nearly any item from this book would enhance a cheese board. The trick is pairing complementary items with the components you choose. Place anything spreadable or syrupy in little ramekins or bowls; include a few complementary nuts and cheeses; add bread or crackers; and meats, vegetables, and fresh or dried fruits. Try to include several elements you want to eat together in one bite. For example: pickled mango (page 227), Manchego, Marcona almonds, and crisp sourdough crackers.

Recipes from this book that don't belong on a cheese board are: coconut shrimp, vinaigrette, sesame ginger sauce, orange supremes, and passion fruit curd.

Fool

Preparing a fool is the easiest way to put a sweet component to use. See page 270 for the specifics, but you essentially just whip cream, fold in a sweet topping, and voilà. If you like a little crunch, add cookie crumbles. Any fruit from this book (other than pickled mango) will work great.

Vegetables

You're probably familiar with that old chef's aphorism: When you've got really good produce, you should do as little as possible to it. I'm generally a big fan of minimally prepared vegetables. Who doesn't love perfectly sautéed broccoli, steamed asparagus with a little drizzle of balsamic, or buttery baked winter squash? But this book's vegetable section takes a different tack, because sometimes more is more. Here, you'll find only bold, exciting vegetable flavors.

You'll do great if you stick with the recipes in this section, but you can also experiment with transforming other vegetables into super-flavorful components by asking yourself 4 questions. In fact, these are the four questions I asked myself when coming up with the 10 component recipes in this chapter:

1. How can I concentrate this vegetable's flavor?

To concentrate a vegetable's flavor, you want to eliminate much of its moisture. For example, caramelized tomatoes (page 101) are baked until their juices thicken to a syrup, and garlicky mushrooms (page 77) are sautéed until their moisture evaporates so they brown and crisp, which makes them twice as flavorful and textured.

2. How can I caramelize it?

Often the process of reducing the moisture content of a vegetable naturally results in caramelization. Sometimes, you just want to caramelize a vegetable without reducing its moisture. For example, grilled corn (page 45) gets a quick char on the grill, heightening its sweetness without dehydrating it. You can do the same with broccoli, Brussels sprouts, or asparagus.

3. How can I add more flavor to it?

Consider adding spices, dried herbs, and flavorful pastes (think: gochujang, harissa, or pesto) to bring out complementary flavors in your vegetable. For instance, miso sweet

potatoes (page 93) are coated in miso butter, and za'atar cauliflower (page 37) is coated in a slurry of za'atar oil and roasted with raisins and Parmesan cheese. Look through your pantry and think about which ingredients can add a little extra something to what you're cooking.

4. How can I add some acidity?

If your vegetable isn't super acidic to begin with, think about adding a little vinegar, citrus juice, or sumac to give it some tartness. Case in point: Beets are a little drab on their own, so I marinate them in red wine vinegar to add kick and tang (page 29).

Not all vegetables will benefit from each of these 4 strategies, and you don't need to use them all in combination. Try what sounds good to you, and skip what doesn't. Most of the vegetables in the recipes that follow use a combination of one or two of my strategies. At the end of the day, sometimes doing nothing really is best when your ingredients are perfect flavor bombs, as in the case of the leafy herbs on page 69.

Marinated beets

Some folks will just never like beets, and that's OK. But if you've written them off due to a fuzzy memory of what they tasted like at a salad bar 10 years ago, then it might be time to try them again. These marinated beets are a great recipe to start you on your beet journey; their sweet-tangy profile converted many a holdout while I was developing the recipe.

Makes 4½ cups [750 g] beets, enough to make all 3 recipes in this section

2 lb [910 g] beets, scrubbed
3 Tbsp red wine vinegar
2 Tbsp extra-virgin olive oil
2 garlic cloves, crushed through a press
1½ tsp dried thyme
¾ tsp salt
¼ tsp freshly ground black pepper
½ tsp ground coriander seeds (optional)

Set a stockpot of water over high heat. Once boiling, add the beets, lower the heat to medium, and simmer, uncovered, for about 45 minutes, until the beets are tender.

Drain, run some cold water over them, drain again, and let them sit for about 5 minutes in a pot of cold water. Once cool enough to handle, use a paper towel to slip the skins off.

Slice the peeled beets into ½ in [13 mm] wedges and/or ⅛ in [3 mm] slices, and place in a mixing bowl. Top with the vinegar, olive oil, garlic, thyme, salt, pepper, and coriander seeds, if using, and toss together. Let sit in the refrigerator for 30 minutes, toss together one more time, and serve.

Storage
After the initial marination, store, covered, in the refrigerator for up to 6 days. Or freeze in an airtight container for at least 3 months. To thaw, place in the refrigerator overnight. Frozen-then-thawed beets will have a softer texture (use them in recipes such as the beet Reubens on page 32 or well-red chopped salad on page 34, where other ingredients have plenty of crunch and chew to compensate).

Store-bought alternatives
Starting this recipe with vacuum-sealed beets from the refrigerated produce section saves a lot of prep time. But look for ones that are just plain beets if you plan to marinate them—canned or pickled varieties won't work here, as they're quite salty and acidic to begin with. But you can use your favorite store-bought pickled beets in any of the recipes that call for marinated beets in this section.

Ways to use:
— In a beet Reuben (page 32)
— For labneh with marinated beets (page 30)
— In a well-red chopped salad (page 34)
— Instead of radishes on a sabzi khordan platter (page 70)
— In place of all or some of the orange supremes in the spinach salad on page 238
— Atop a plate of garlicky hummus (page 64) for herby, earthy tanginess
— As a salad composé with beets, goat cheese, and pistachios

Labneh with marinated beets

Labneh is simply yogurt that's been strained until it's much thicker in texture. If you don't feel like straining your own, simply use store-bought Greek yogurt instead to turn this into a recipe requiring zero active time. But don't try straining Greek yogurt to make labneh. It's already quite strained, and straining it further results in a chalky texture. The best starting point is a plain, unstrained yogurt with a flavor you love. You can also drizzle labneh with a little olive oil and serve with pita or crudités.

⏱ **5+ MIN**
⊖ 15+ MIN
◔ 30+ MIN

4 to 6 servings as an appetizer

1 qt [960 g] plain yogurt
1 garlic clove, crushed through
  a press
¼ tsp salt
Freshly ground black pepper
**1¾ cups [290 g] marinated beets
  (page 29)**
Extra-virgin olive oil, for drizzling

Set a fine-mesh sieve over a large bowl so that it rests with 1 to 2 in [2.5 to 5 cm] of space between the bottom of the sieve and the bottom of the bowl. Place the yogurt in the sieve, cover, and refrigerate for at least 12 hours. It should give off about half its volume in whey.

Discard the whey from the bowl and place the yogurt in the emptied bowl. Add the garlic, salt, and a pinch of pepper. Mix together and place in a serving bowl. Top with the beets and a drizzle of olive oil.

Other components you can use
Labneh is also delicious topped with caramelized tomatoes (page 101) and grilled corn (page 45). Or you could top it with coarsely chopped leafy herbs (page 69), pistachios, and a little extra olive oil. Or try some roasted grapes (page 219) and balsamic glaze for a totally different flavor.

Beet Reubens

There's a little sandwich shop near our apartment in Melbourne called Rusty's, and they make a mean vegan Reuben with beets (in place of corned beef). This recipe, in all its melting magenta cheese glory, takes its inspiration from Rusty's version. To make it vegan like the original, leave out the Worcestershire and substitute vegan mayonnaise, vegan butter, and any sliced vegan cheese that melts well.

⊘ 5+ MIN
⊖ **15+ MIN**
ⓘ 30+ MIN

4 sandwiches

For the Russian dressing:
½ cup [115 g] mayonnaise
2 Tbsp ketchup
2 tsp dried onion flakes
1½ tsp jarred horseradish
1 tsp hot sauce
1 dash Worcestershire sauce
1 tsp paprika
¼ tsp freshly ground black pepper

For the sandwiches:
1⅓ cups [205 g] marinated beet slices (page 29), well drained
8 slices dark rye bread
3 Tbsp unsalted butter, at room temperature
8 slices Swiss
¾ cup [100 g] sauerkraut, well drained

To make the dressing, in a small mixing bowl, whisk together the mayonnaise, ketchup, onion flakes, horseradish, hot sauce, Worcestershire sauce, paprika, and pepper. Set aside.

To assemble the sandwiches, slice the beets (if they aren't already sliced). Place the slices of bread on a cutting board. Butter the slices and flip them over so you don't see the buttered sides. Place a slice of cheese on each one. Spread about 1 Tbsp of the Russian dressing on each piece of cheese. Place about 3 Tbsp of the sauerkraut and ⅓ cup [50 g] of the beet slices on 4 of the bread slices. Top with the remaining 4 bread slices.

Set a nonstick sauté pan over medium heat. Once hot, place two sandwiches in the pan, and place another pan on top to create a little pressure. Flip after about 3 minutes, place the other pan on top again, and let sear for another 3 minutes. The bread should be toasted but not burnt, the cheese should be melted, and the sandwiches should be warmed through. Repeat with the remaining sandwiches. Slice each in half and serve.

Recipe note
Make sure you place the cheese against the bread—that way it will melt better, and will create a barrier to keep the bread from getting soggy.

Make-ahead instructions
Marinate the beets and make the Russian dressing up to 3 days ahead of time, and assemble and grill the sandwiches at the last minute.

Substitutions
Use corned beef in place of the beets for a classic Reuben.

Well-red chopped salad

This entirely reddish-purple salad looks one-note but tastes incredibly complex. There's such a big difference between my expectations and experience of it, and I love that little bit of surprise.

———————

To make the dressing, in a small mixing bowl or jar, smash the beet slices with a fork against the side of the bowl. Top with the olive oil, vinegar, honey, and salt and mix to combine.

To make the salad, tear the radicchio into pieces and place in a salad bowl or mixing bowl. Add the red onion and toss with about half of the dressing until evenly coated. Top with the beets, olives, blood oranges, feta, and the rest of the dressing, and rustle it a little with the tongs just so the feta becomes a little pink (but don't fold it or the ingredients will fall to the bottom). Serve immediately.

⏱ 5+ MIN
◷ 15+ MIN
ⓘ **30+ MIN**

6 servings

For the dressing:
2 marinated beet slices (page 29)
¼ cup [55 g] extra-virgin olive oil
1 Tbsp red wine vinegar
1 tsp honey
¼ tsp salt

For the salad:
1 medium or 2 small heads radicchio
¼ red onion, thinly sliced
1½ cups [250 g] marinated beets (page 29), well drained
½ cup [70 g] pitted kalamata olives
4 blood oranges, supremed (see page 235)
½ cup [70 g] crumbled feta

Make-ahead instructions
Make the dressing up to 2 days ahead of time, wash the radicchio and store as on page 69 for 2 to 3 days, supreme the oranges the day before, and prep and assemble the salad in its entirety at the last minute.

Other components you can use
Replace some or all of the blood oranges with roasted grapes (page 219) or mulled wine pears (page 243).

Za'atar cauliflower

There are two things you need to know about za'atar (often translated as "wild thyme"): First, rather than mixing up your own with French thyme, you should always buy the real deal from a Middle Eastern market or the international aisle of the supermarket. French thyme and za'atar share little more than a common English name.

And second, always be generous when using za'atar. Think of manakish za'atar, a flatbread topped with such a thick slurry of za'atar oil that its surface looks like a lush, mossy forest. Manakish za'atar inspired this way of preparing cauliflower, which is coated in an entire cup of za'atar and a quarter cup of olive oil. Don't cut back on either, and take the time to fully coat each piece using your hands.

———

Makes about 6 cups [800 g], enough to make any 1 recipe from this section

1 head cauliflower
¼ cup [55 g] extra-virgin olive oil
1 cup [110 g] za'atar
½ tsp salt
½ cup [45 g] coarsely grated Parmesan or Pecorino Romano
½ cup [75 g] raisins or sultanas

Preheat the oven to 425°F [220°C].

Cut the cauliflower into florets and place on a rimmed sheet pan. Combine the oil and za'atar in a small mixing bowl, then spoon the mixture over the cauliflower. Use your hands to coat the cauliflower evenly with the za'atar slurry (pack it on so it sticks). Once evenly coated, spread into an even layer with space between the florets (do not crowd the sheet pan). Sprinkle evenly with the salt and cheese.

Roast for about 15 minutes, until the cauliflower has softened but is still somewhat firm. Sprinkle on the raisins and roast for 3 more minutes, until they puff up and caramelize lightly. Keep a close eye on them and make sure they don't burn.

Recipe notes
Do not use French thyme (see headnote). If you double or triple this recipe, use multiple sheet pans.

Storage
Cauliflower keeps in the fridge for a day or two, but roasted cauliflower is better frozen, and will last for at least 3 months in the freezer in a tightly sealed container. Freeze in a single layer, then transfer to a tightly sealed bag.

Ways to use:
— Dress it simply (page 38)
— In cauliflower lentil salad (page 40)
— For cauliflower burritos (page 42)
— Make a grain bowl (page 96) with za'atar cauliflower and cilantro lime dressing (page 147)
— Try serving za'atar chickpeas with yellow rice (page 202) with some za'atar cauliflower on the side. It's delicious with tzatziki (page 199).
— Add some za'atar cauliflower to an antipasto platter or cheese board
— Make a focaccia topped with za'atar cauliflower and cheese

Za'atar cauliflower, dressed up

While you can absolutely serve the za'atar cauliflower on page 37 on its own as a side, it's even more delicious with a little tahini sauce and some fresh cilantro.

⊘ **5+ MIN**
⊖ 15+ MIN
ⓘ 30+ MIN

4 servings as a side

⅓ cup [85 g] tahini
⅓ cup [80 g] water
¼ cup [60 g] lemon juice
1 garlic clove, crushed through
   a press
Salt
1 batch za'atar cauliflower
   (page 37)
½ cup [20 g] packed fresh cilantro
   leaves

Place the tahini, water, lemon juice, garlic, and a pinch of salt in a small mixing bowl. Whisk the mixture until smooth (it will start out looking very thin and broken, then will thicken and smooth out).

Place the za'atar cauliflower in a bowl, drizzle with the tahini sauce, sprinkle with the cilantro, then serve with more tahini sauce at the table.

Substitutions
You can use fresh basil or parsley instead of cilantro, or really any leafy herb from page 69.

Cauliflower lentil salad

The key to this salad is to cook your lentils perfectly and then rinse them. If you cook them too long, they'll start to fall apart, and will make the dressing starchy and gloopy. If you cook them too little, they'll taste unpleasantly raw. Cook them just enough, and you've got a delicious salad that works great as a vegetarian main or side.

———

Boil the lentils according to their package instructions (times vary by variety) until fluffy and soft but not yet falling apart. Once they're done, rinse and drain them well, then place in a mixing bowl.

In a small mixing bowl, whisk together the olive oil, vinegar, mustard, garlic, za'atar, and salt. Set aside.

Add the arugula, onion, and dressing to the bowl with the lentils. Toss together until evenly coated. Add the cauliflower and feta, toss gently, and enjoy.

⊘ 5+ MIN
⊖ **15+ MIN**
ⓘ 30+ MIN

8 to 10 servings

1½ cups [285 g] brown or green
   lentils
¼ cup [55 g] extra-virgin olive oil
2 Tbsp balsamic vinegar
1 Tbsp brown mustard
2 garlic cloves, crushed through
   a press
1 Tbsp za'atar
½ tsp salt
2 big handfuls arugula
1 small or ½ large red onion, very
   thinly sliced
**1 batch za'atar cauliflower
   (page 37), chilled**
1 cup [140 g] crumbled feta

Make-ahead instructions
You can make the lentils, dressing, and cauliflower the day before, then bring everything together to serve.

Cauliflower burritos

The za'atar cauliflower packs such a punch, you don't need to add much more to make a delicious burrito. Cilantro lime rice, black beans, a little salsa, and some stretchy cheese round out every bite.

⏱ 5+ MIN
◔ 15+ MIN
ⓘ **30+ MIN**

8 burritos

1 cup [200 g] medium-grain rice
1¼ cups [295 g] water, plus more
  for rinsing
½ tsp salt
½ cup [20 g] chopped fresh
  cilantro
1 Tbsp lime juice
½ tsp lime zest
8 large flour tortillas
1 batch za'atar cauliflower
  (page 37)
3 cups [195 g] shredded cabbage
One 15 oz [425 g] can black beans,
  drained and rinsed
1½ cups [165 g] shredded
  mozzarella or Monterey Jack
1 cup [235 g] salsa (page 163,
  or store-bought), plus more
  for serving
Hot sauce, as needed
1 small or ½ large red onion, very
  thinly sliced

Place the rice in a small saucepan. Cover with some cold water, swish around well, and drain. Add the rice back to the saucepan and stir in the water and salt. Place over medium-high heat with the lid off (do not stir again). As soon as the rice comes to a simmer, cover with the lid and lower the heat to low.

Simmer, covered, for 15 minutes without peeking and without stirring. After 15 minutes, without uncovering the pan, remove from the heat and rest the rice for at least 10 minutes (up to 30). Sprinkle with the cilantro, lime juice, and lime zest and fluff with a fork to combine completely.

Place one tortilla on a plate in the microwave, and microwave for just a few seconds until warm (this will make it more flexible so it won't tear as you roll it, but don't heat it too long or it will become brittle). You can also warm tortillas in an ungreased skillet or over a gas flame.

Top the tortilla with about ¾ cup [100 g] cauliflower, ⅓ cup [60 g] rice, ⅓ cup [25 g] cabbage, 3 Tbsp beans, 3 Tbsp mozzarella, 2 Tbsp salsa, hot sauce, if using, and some sliced onion. Fold the sides in around the filling, then roll from bottom to top while putting pressure on the sides. Wrap tightly in aluminum foil. Repeat with the remaining tortillas.

Place a skillet over medium-low heat. Once hot, add two foil-wrapped burritos. Flip after about 2 minutes, and repeat on the other sides. Remove from the heat once they're toasted and warmed through, and repeat with the other burritos. (The more layers of foil you used, the longer it will take to cook.) Serve with extra salsa, unwrapping as you take bites to keep your burrito held together.

Make-ahead instructions
After wrapping in aluminum foil, place the burritos in a sealable container and freeze. To thaw, bake from frozen (in foil) on a small rimmed sheet pan in a 450°F [230°C] oven or toaster oven for 1 hour. If you're in a hurry, you can remove from the foil and microwave for about 5 minutes until thawed and heated through (rewrap in foil afterward, if you prefer).

Grilled corn

Charring your corn adds a lovely smoky note and tempers its sweetness. Grill as many or as few ears as you'd like: Roast a single ear of corn on a gas stove, or grill a dozen at once on your outdoor grill. I like making a big batch and freezing the leftovers (see Storage)—it adds a big splash of summer flavor to winter dishes.

Makes 9 ears or 6¾ cups [945 g] kernels, enough to make all 3 recipes in this section

9 shucked ears of corn
An outdoor grill or a gas stove

To grill with gas outdoors: Let your grill preheat on high. Once the grates are hot, place the corn on the grill.

To grill with charcoal outdoors: To be efficient with your charcoal, it's best to plan to grill a couple other things at a lower temperature after your corn is done. For example, start the corn on high heat at the beginning, move on to other vegetables, then move on to chicken (butterflied or parts) once the heat has died down a bit.

To roast with a gas stovetop indoors: Turn your largest gas burner to high heat. Use metal tongs to place 1 or 2 ears of corn right on the grate. Be very careful, and don't get distracted. Work in batches until they're all done.

Rotate the ears frequently and keep a close eye on them. Remove as soon as they are about 50% charred on all sides. Let cool before slicing the kernels from the cob.

Easier alternative
You can use plain frozen corn in any of the recipes in this section, especially when fresh corn is out of season in the winter and spring.

Storage
Whole grilled ears of corn will keep for up to 3 days in the fridge. Kernels will keep for 2 days in the fridge before they become starchy. To store for at least 3 months, cut the kernels off the cob after grilling, place in a freezer bag, push out as much air as possible, and freeze flat. Corn starts to lose sweetness as soon as it's harvested, so try to prep and freeze it as soon as you bring it home.

Ways to use:
— As elotes preparados on page 46
— Atop the bruschetta on page 48
— In the spicy sweet potato corn chowder on page 50
— To add to the cornmeal pancake stack on page 106
— Layer into the summer strata on page 104 instead of fresh corn
— Make the pizza bianca ai funghi on page 82, replacing half of the mushrooms with grilled corn
— Use in the Southwestern cobb salad on page 152
— Drizzle grilled corn on the cob with gochujang sauce (page 181)
— Add to a grain bowl (page 96)

For a summer-special, mixed grill meal:
— Before you start grilling your corn, grill some potatoes (halved, coated lightly in oil and salt), then grill skewers of marinated shrimp alongside the corn and serve all together
— Fill your favorite tacos: Make the avocado tomatillo salsa verde on page 163, sear some carne asada, chop up some onions and cilantro, and use all this to top warmed corn tortillas—and don't forget the lime wedges!
— Make a simple corn salad with tomatoes, feta, parsley, and actually good vinaigrette (page 139)

Elotes preparados

When I grill a bunch of corn, I almost always make elotes preparados. You can easily double, triple, or quadruple the recipe, depending on whether you're making a snack or feeding a crowd. This recipe is so easy, if I say another word about it in this headnote, I'll give away the whole thing.

⏱ **5+ MIN**
◔ 15+ MIN
◷ 30+ MIN

4 servings

4 ears grilled corn (page 45)
¼ cup [60 g] mayonnaise
⅔ cup [100 g] crumbled Cotija
Cayenne pepper
Salt
4 lime wedges

Brush the grilled corn with the mayo, sprinkle with the Cotija, and add cayenne and salt to taste. Serve with lime wedges on the side.

Recipe note
If you're working with kernels, make esquites instead. Dress grilled (or sautéed frozen) kernels with a little mayo, lime juice, Cotija, cayenne, and salt to taste.

Substitutions
For a twist, use feta and toum (page 171) instead of Cotija and mayo.

Grilled corn and tomato bruschetta

A late summer treat, if ever there was one: garlic toast topped with grilled sweet corn and fresh tomatoes, and as much basil as possible.

———

⏱ 5+ MIN
◐ 15+ MIN
ⓘ 30+ MIN

35 to 40 pieces

4 tomatoes
1½ cups [210 g] grilled corn kernels (page 45)
2 Tbsp extra-virgin olive oil
2 Tbsp balsamic vinegar
1 small bunch fresh basil, leaves torn
1 garlic clove, crushed through a press, plus 2 or 3 garlic cloves, halved crosswise
½ tsp salt
¼ tsp freshly ground black pepper
1 large baguette, sliced ¾ in [2 cm] thick

Coarsely chop the tomatoes and place in a medium mixing bowl. Stir in the corn, olive oil, vinegar, basil, crushed garlic, salt, and pepper. Let sit for at least 15 minutes, until the tomatoes have given off some juices.

Toast a batch of baguette slices until well done but not burnt. As soon as they come out of the toaster, rub each slice with a halved garlic clove and place on a serving plate. Scoop up the tomato-corn mixture with a slotted spoon and top the toast. Work in batches and serve each batch right away.

Make-ahead instructions
Fold together the marinated tomato-corn mixture, refrigerate overnight, toast the bread at the last minute, and assemble the moment before serving.

Substitutions
If it's not late summer, use sautéed frozen corn kernels and caramelize the tomatoes (see page 101). Dice or lightly smash the caramelized tomatoes, and use about half the olive oil, vinegar, and salt (to taste).

Spicy sweet potato corn chowder

Any recipe that involves cheese, hot sauce, corn, and sweet potatoes is going to be a winner. If you've got grilled corn in the freezer, this recipe works great all winter long, but you can otherwise use frozen corn kernels. It won't have that same charred flavor, but will still be delicious.

———————

Heat a large stockpot or Dutch oven over medium heat for a few minutes. Add the olive oil, followed immediately by the onion and a little salt to taste (about ¼ tsp). Cook for about 10 minutes, stirring occasionally.

Add the flour, paprika, pepper, and turmeric and stir together for about 30 seconds. Add the stock and garlic and whisk together until smooth. Bring to a simmer over medium-high heat, whisking occasionally, add the corn and sweet potato, wait for it to come back up to a simmer, cover, and lower the heat to medium-low to maintain a simmer for about 8 minutes, until the sweet potato is tender.

Add the half-and-half and sriracha, then gradually sprinkle in the Cheddar, whisking constantly until the cheese melts. Taste and season with more salt if necessary (this will vary, depending on how salty your stock is).

Serve in bowls and top with more sriracha if you'd like it to be extra spicy. Garnish with cilantro, as needed.

⏱ 5+ MIN
⊝ 15+ MIN
ⓘ **30+ MIN**

5 servings

2 Tbsp extra-virgin olive oil
1 onion, diced
Salt
⅓ cup [45 g] all-purpose flour
2 tsp ground paprika
1 tsp freshly ground black pepper
1 tsp ground turmeric
6 cups [1.4 liters] chicken or
  vegetable stock
3 garlic cloves, crushed through
  a press
**3½ cups [500 g] grilled corn
  kernels (page 45)**
3½ cups [400 g] medium-diced
  peeled sweet potato
1 cup [235 g] half-and-half
3 Tbsp sriracha, plus more
  for serving
1 cup [130 g] heaped shredded
  Cheddar
Fresh cilantro leaves, for garnish
  (optional)

Make-ahead instructions
This soup keeps for about 3 days in the fridge, or for at least 3 months in tightly sealed containers in the freezer.

Smoky eggplant

There are essentially two ways to cook eggplant: 1) quickly, to char it and let it cook just to a toothsome texture, or 2) for-absolute-ever, until it shrinks down into a smoky eggplant paste. While the first is best in salads, pastas, and as a veggie side, the second has unparalleled flavor.

This eggplant is fire-roasted, then oven-roasted to cara-melize and cook down. The result: silky strips of eggplant that are fully infused with smoky flavor.

_____

Makes just over 3 cups [725 g], enough to make all 3 recipes in this section

15 small Italian eggplants [3 kg], left whole and pricked once with a fork
Olive oil, for drizzling
Salt

Recipe note
For indoor grilling, set a gas stove to high heat. Open a window and turn on the exhaust. Place an eggplant directly on the grate. Let it blacken and become wrinkly on one side, then rotate it until it's wrinkly all over (about 8 minutes total). Repeat with the rest.

Storage
Smoky eggplant will keep in the refrigerator for about 4 days, or sealed tightly in the freezer for at least 3 months without loss of quality.

Ways to use:
— For baba ganoush (page 54)
— In eggplant ricotta frittata (page 56)
— Top Chicago-style deep-dish pizza with smoky eggplant and basil (page 58)
— Use a few strips of eggplant in place of the mushrooms on a pizza bianca (page 82)
— Tuck into an omelette (page 78)
— Layer into your favorite lasagna

Outdoor grilling instructions (see recipe note for indoor instructions): Set your grill to high heat with the lid closed for a few minutes. Place your eggplants on the grates and close the lid. Rotate them as they blacken on one side, and repeat until wrinkly and blackened all over (10 to 20 minutes for smaller ones, longer for larger ones). Transfer to a large plate.

Strip the charred eggplant skins as soon as they come off the grill (be careful and use gloves, or wait for them to cool). The skins should come off in big strips, leaving behind golden brown flesh underneath. Hold the eggplants by the stems and use the side of a paring knife and your thumb to get the strips started. Place the stripped eggplants in a large bowl, leaving the skins behind on the plate to discard.

Preheat the oven to 450°F [230°C]. Line 1 or 2 rimmed sheet pans with parchment.

Spit the eggplants in half lengthwise and cut off the stems. If any are too soft to slice, spread them open a bit with your fingers, so the inside is exposed.

Place the eggplants cut-side up on the sheet pan(s), leaving any liquid behind in the bowl. Don't crowd the pan, and use both pans if necessary. Drizzle each with about 1 Tbsp of olive oil and sprinkle with ½ to ¾ tsp salt.

Roast for about 50 minutes. They're done once they've shrunk down, turned golden brown, and the juices have cooked off. Let cool on the sheet pan and then remove to a container to store.

Baba ganoush

Water is baba ganoush's nemesis, and eggplant has a ton of it. There are lots of ways cooks go about eliminating water from baba ganoush, but this section's double-roasting method might just be the most flavor-packed. Roasting charred eggplant in the oven concentrates its flavors, resulting in a super creamy and rich baba ganoush.

———

Place the garlic in a food processor fitted with the blade attachment. Process until the garlic is minced. Add the eggplant, lemon juice, parsley, tahini, and a pinch of salt and pulse a few times, just until it's creamy but not completely smooth.

Spread onto a plate or bowl, top with a drizzle of extra-virgin olive oil, a little more parsley, and a pinch of sea salt, if using.

⏱ **5+ MIN**
◐ 15+ MIN
◔ 30+ MIN

About 2 cups [500 g]

1 or 2 garlic cloves
1⅔ cups [380 g] smoky eggplant (page 53)
¼ cup [60 g] lemon juice
¼ cup [10 g] chopped fresh parsley, plus more for garnish
3 Tbsp tahini
Salt
Extra-virgin olive oil, for drizzling
Sea salt (optional)

Recipe notes
You can skip the food processor, crush the garlic through a press, and mash the rest of the ingredients with the back of a fork in a bowl. Serve with a handful of pomegranate seeds if you're feeling fancy, and enjoy along with pita and kofta to make it a hearty meal.

Make-ahead instructions
Baba ganoush keeps for about 4 days in the fridge, or for at least 3 months tightly sealed in the freezer. Thaw overnight in the refrigerator.

Substitutions
You can omit the parsley if you're making this on a whim and don't have any handy. It's not the same, but it's still super delicious.

Eggplant ricotta frittata

The best frittatas are a little top-heavy on the stuff-to-eggs ratio. This frittata's eggs are outweighed by silky, smoky eggplant strips, juicy cherry tomatoes, and gobs of creamy ricotta. Frittata possibilities are endless. In fact, a ricotta frittata is a great way to use up almost any veggie component in this book, if you don't mind getting a little creative.

⏱ 5+ MIN
◔ **15+ MIN**
🕙 30+ MIN

4 to 6 servings

6 large eggs
1 garlic clove, crushed through a press
1 small handful whole fresh chives, plus more for garnish
½ tsp salt
½ tsp freshly ground black pepper
Extra-virgin olive oil, for cooking
½ cup [115 g] smoky eggplant (page 53)
⅔ cup [100 g] cherry tomatoes, halved
½ cup [120 g] full-fat ricotta
Sea salt (optional)

Preheat the broiler to its highest setting and set a rack below it with enough room for a pan. Let it preheat for just 5 to 10 minutes—most broilers shut off once the oven reaches temperature.

In a mixing bowl, whisk together the eggs, garlic, chives, salt, and pepper. Set aside.

Set a 10 in [25 cm] broiler-proof nonstick or cast-iron skillet over medium heat. Once hot, add about 1 Tbsp of oil, swirl to coat, and add the egg mixture. Give it a quick scramble to form a few big curds, and then remove from the heat while it's set on the bottom but still very runny on top. Top with the eggplant, tomatoes, and dollops of ricotta.

Place under the broiler for about 10 minutes (this will vary from oven to oven, so keep a very close eye on it) until puffy around the edges and cooked through in the center. Top with more chives and a nice pinch of sea salt, if using, and serve immediately.

Substitutions
You can use a packed ¼ cup [10 g] of fresh basil or cilantro in place of the chives. Substitute any fresh cheese in place of the ricotta, but cut back on the amount for stronger flavors, such as goat cheese. If you've got them on hand, you can replace the fresh tomatoes with a smaller amount of caramelized tomatoes (page 101).

Other components you can use
Replace the eggplant with za'atar cauliflower (page 37), garlicky mushrooms (page 77), or grilled corn (page 45).

Chicago-style deep-dish pizza

I grew up in the Chicago area, but haven't lived there in over a decade. This pizza recipe has gotten me through many bouts of homesickness, and is inspired by my favorite deep dish, Lou Malnati's. They certainly don't make their crust with beer, but I find that it's the best way to replicate their distinctive crust at home. You can use whatever beer you have on hand, as long as it's not too hoppy, bitter, or sour—these characteristics will come through strongly in the finished dough and throw off the overall flavor of the pizza.

———————

⏲ 5+ MIN
◔ 15+ MIN
ⓘ **30+ MIN**

6 servings

For the dough:
¾ cup [175 g] beer, at room
    temperature
1½ tsp instant or active dry yeast
1 tsp sugar
2 cups [260 g] all-purpose flour
3 Tbsp polenta or cornmeal
2 Tbsp extra-virgin olive oil,
    plus more for greasing the pan
1 tsp salt

For the pizza:
8 oz [225 g] shredded or sliced
    mozzarella
3 garlic cloves, crushed through
    a press
1 small bunch fresh basil
Salt
**1 cup [230 g] smoky eggplant
    (page 53)**
1 cup [240 g] tomato sauce
½ cup [25 g] finely grated
    Parmesan

To make the dough, combine the beer, yeast, and sugar in the bowl of a stand mixer fitted with the dough hook attachment. Stir until the yeast dissolves. Add the flour, polenta, olive oil, and salt and stir together with the dough hook at low speed. Once the dough comes together into a shaggy ball, increase the speed to medium-high and knead until smooth and elastic, about 5 minutes. The dough should pool slightly at the bottom, but will pull away from the sides of the bowl after a couple minutes.

Once the dough smooths out, oil one hand and scrape the dough off the hook and back into the bowl. Cover the bowl with a plate and set it aside for about 3 hours in a very warm spot in your kitchen. It's done rising once it's doubled in size.

Once the dough is ready, preheat the oven to 450°F [230°C].

To make the pizza, generously oil a 10 in [25 cm] cast-iron skillet. Coat your fingers in oil, scrape the dough into the skillet, and work it into a thin layer that goes all the way up the sides of the skillet.

Sprinkle the cheese on top of the dough, followed by the garlic and basil. Season with a little pinch of salt and arrange the smoky eggplant slices in a single layer. Dollop the tomato sauce evenly over the top, then spread the sauce out. Sprinkle on the Parmesan.

Bake for about 25 minutes directly on the floor of your oven (not on a rack). The pizza is done once the crust is browned around the edges and golden-brown underneath, the cheese is stringy, and the top is caramelized.

Let the pizza cool in the pan for about 10 minutes before serving. Slice and serve out of the pan.

Make-ahead instructions

You can make the dough a day or two before. Let it rise at room temperature for 2 hours, then refrigerate the ball of dough in a bowl covered with plastic wrap (you can use it right from the refrigerator). Or freeze it for months: Let it rise at room temperature for 3 hours, then punch it down, place in a resealable bag with room for expansion, and freeze solid. Thaw in the refrigerator overnight when you're ready to use it.

Substitutions

In place of the beer, measure 1 Tbsp of apple cider vinegar and top it off with water to end up with ¾ cup [175 g] total. In place of the fresh basil, use 1 Tbsp dried. This pizza dough is absolutely worth the effort, but 1 lb [455 g] of store-bought pizza dough will work in a pinch. Also feel free to use store-bought tomato sauce if you don't have a favorite recipe.

Other components you can use

In place of the eggplant: garlicky mushrooms (page 77) or turkey spinach meatballs (page 119). Don't overdo it with the toppings; choose just one and place it in a single layer with a bit of breathing room.

Whole roasted garlic

You can get so many different flavors out of a simple head of garlic, depending on how you cook it. Roasting is best when you want to add a lot of garlic flavor without any harsh bite—though I usually include a clove or two of fresh when cooking with roasted, just to add a little sharpness back in.

———

Makes 1½ cups [375 g] smashed, enough to make all 3 recipes in this section

10 to 12 whole garlic heads
1½ Tbsp extra-virgin olive oil
½ tsp salt

Preheat the oven to 375°F [190°C].

Slice just the top off of each garlic head, exposing the cloves like honeycomb (save any large chunks sliced off). Peel away any loose outer skins from the garlic heads, being careful to leave the cloves intact. Peel away and discard any cloves that look rotten. Place the little bits and cut-side-up heads in a small baking dish. Drizzle evenly with the olive oil and use your hands to coat evenly, then sprinkle with the salt. Cover the baking dish with aluminum foil and tightly seal it on two sides.

Bake for about 75 minutes, until the cloves are golden brown and easily pierced with a fork. Let cool for at least 15 minutes, then squeeze the cloves out of their paper skins.

Recipe note
You can make as much garlic as you'd like at once, even an entire sheet pan, as long as they all fit in a single layer. Scale up or down as necessary.

Storage
Whole roasted garlic lasts in the fridge for 3 to 4 days, or tightly sealed in the freezer for at least 3 months with no loss of quality.

Ways to use:
— Slather on garlic bread (page 62)
— Make some garlicky hummus (page 64)
— Fold into spaghetti aglio e olio (page 66)
— Mix into buttermilk mashed potatoes (see page 124) in place of the garlic you simmer alongside the potatoes
— Serve a few cloves over your favorite grilled veggies, along with actually good vinaigrette (page 139)
— Serve bread with a plate of olive oil, sea salt, balsamic vinegar, and roasted garlic
— Spread fig jam and roasted garlic on toast with a little sprinkling of fresh thyme leaves

Garlic bread

One of the most beautiful things about roasted garlic is its spreadable texture, which makes it ideal for garlic bread. You can totally use a smaller amount of garlic powder instead for a similar effect if you don't have roasted garlic on hand, but real roasted garlic is well worth the extra roasting time.

———

⏱ **5+ MIN**
◔ 15+ MIN
ⓘ 30+ MIN

6 servings as an appetizer

1 large ciabatta loaf
½ cup [125 g] whole roasted garlic (page 61)
2 garlic cloves, crushed through a press
3 Tbsp extra-virgin olive oil or unsalted butter, at room temperature
½ cup [30 g] finely grated Parmesan, plus more for sprinkling
¼ cup [10 g] minced fresh parsley
¾ tsp sea salt

Preheat the oven to 350°F [180°C].

Place a long sheet of aluminum foil on a sheet pan, and place the ciabatta on top of it. Slice the ciabatta every ¾ in [2 cm], but don't slice all the way through, leaving the loaf intact on the bottom.

In a small bowl, mix together the roasted garlic, fresh garlic, olive oil, Parmesan, parsley, and salt. Smash together until the cloves mostly dissolve into the oil. Spread this mixture between the bread slices. Sprinkle about 1 Tbsp of Parmesan on top, then wrap the loaf in the foil.

Bake for about 15 minutes, and serve right out of the oven.

Recipe note
If your loaf of bread is extremely flat, you can slice it down the middle, hot dog–style, instead.

Garlicky hummus

To everyone who's ever had the self-destructive urge to add two or three entire heads of garlic to a batch of hummus, this recipe gets you. Roasted garlic is the secret to adding a ton of garlic flavor without too much harshness. It's still important to add a single clove of raw garlic, just for a little bite, but this hummus's deep, sweet garlic flavor comes from the roasted stuff. This recipe might not take you the full 15 minutes, but if you want to make it a little more substantial, make one of the veggie toppings following the recipe.

⏱ 5+ MIN
◔ **15+ MIN**
ⓘ 30+ MIN

About 3½ cups [900 g]

7 to 9 ice cubes (or ½ cup [115 g] cold water)
1 garlic clove
Two 15 oz [425 g] cans chickpeas, drained and rinsed
½ cup [125 g] whole roasted garlic (page 61)
⅓ cup [85 g] tahini
¼ cup [60 g] lemon juice
Sea salt
Extra-virgin olive oil, for drizzling

Place the ice cubes and raw garlic clove in the bowl of a food processor fitted with the blade attachment. Top with the chickpeas, roasted garlic, tahini, lemon juice, and salt to taste, and blend until completely smooth.

Scoop the hummus onto a couple plates or shallow bowls, and make little dips across the surface with the back of a spoon. Drizzle with olive oil, sprinkle with salt, and enjoy.

Make-ahead instructions
Hummus will keep in the fridge for 3 to 4 days, or the freezer for at least 3 months.

Other components you can use
Top your hummus with marinated beets (page 29) or za'atar cauliflower (page 37), and serve with crudités instead of pita.

Spaghetti aglio e olio

This was the very last recipe I wrote and tested for this book, so I posted a little celebratory photo to Instagram of my computer with the ingredients slightly out of frame. I immediately got a message from a friend, who was alarmed that this aglio e olio recipe seemed to only call for 1 clove of raw garlic. So instead of horrified, I hope you'll be as relieved as my friend was to hear that this recipe actually includes an entire ½ cup [125 g] of roasted garlic in addition to the 1 raw clove. The roasted cloves meld together with the toasted bread crumbs to coat the spaghetti in a layer of crispy, umami goodness.

⟳ 5+ MIN
⊖ 15+ MIN
ⓘ **30+ MIN**

3 to 4 servings

For the bread crumbs:
½ cup [50 g] bread crumbs
2 tsp extra-virgin olive oil
1 garlic clove, crushed through a
   press
Pinch of salt
3 Tbsp finely grated Parmesan
½ tsp freshly ground black pepper
¼ tsp lemon zest
¼ tsp red pepper flakes

For the pasta:
Salt
8 oz [225 g] spaghetti
**½ cup [125 g] whole roasted garlic
   (page 61)**
½ cup [20 g] chopped fresh parsley
¼ cup [55 g] extra-virgin olive oil
1 Tbsp lemon juice

To toast the bread crumbs, place the bread crumbs in a cold sauté pan. Drizzle evenly with the olive oil, add the garlic and salt, and rub the bread crumbs between your fingers until they're very evenly coated in the oil. Set over medium heat and cook, stirring constantly, for 3 to 4 minutes until the bread crumbs smell and look toasted. Transfer immediately to a container. Once they cool down a little, add the Parmesan, black pepper, lemon zest, and red pepper flakes and toss together.

To make the pasta, set a large stockpot full of water over high heat. Add enough salt that it tastes pleasantly salty (like stock). Once it comes to a rolling boil, add the spaghetti and cook to al dente, according to the package instructions. Once it's done, drain the pasta and place it back in the pot. Add the roasted garlic, parsley (reserve some for garnish), olive oil, lemon juice, and half of the bread crumbs. Toss together and move to a serving bowl. Top with the rest of the bread crumbs and remaining parsley, and enjoy.

Make-ahead instructions
You can toast the bread crumbs and store them in the fridge for 2 to 3 days, or freeze for at least 3 months. Roast the garlic ahead of time, then make the spaghetti at the last moment.

Other components you can use
This dish is lovely with a handful of garlicky mushrooms (page 77).

Leafy herbs

Herbs fall into two distinct categories: leafy and woody. Woody herbs, like thyme and rosemary, are incredibly fragrant, but they can become too perfumy when used in large quantities. That's why I usually prefer leafy herbs, like parsley and cilantro. The more the merrier! Use them with reckless abandon, and think of them as flavorful lettuces.

Herbs won't last long stored improperly in unwashed bunches. But if you do a little prep work ahead of time, they'll last for days or weeks. Then you'll have them on hand to enliven just about everything you make.

Buy bunches of a few favorites, such as parsley, cilantro, mint, basil, dill, chives, and green onions. The most adaptable leafy herbs (and the ones most broadly used in this book) are parsley, cilantro, mint, and green onion.

———————

To make all 3 recipes in this section, buy 3 medium bunches of parsley, 2 large bunches of green onions, 2 large bunches of cilantro, 1 large bunch of basil, and 1 large bunch of mint.

To wash and store: For basil and chives, do not wash ahead of time. Basil should be kept with freshly cut stems in a glass of water at cool room temperature. For chives, discard any wilted ones, wrap up the good ones in paper towels in a sealed container, and store in the fridge. Rinse both right before using. If fresh, they should last for a few days.

For parsley, cilantro, mint, dill, and green onions, wash and store in a paper towel–lined container. Stem and discard any damaged leaves (leave green onions whole, strip away any damaged layers, and slice off the roots). Submerge in a salad spinner full of cold water. Swish around, lift out the basket, dump the water, and repeat 2 more times. Spin dry. Spread out a large, clean dish towel (or paper towels). Evenly distribute the herbs, then loosely roll up the towel. Place the bundle in a container, then store in the fridge for up to 2 weeks. This also works great for kale, arugula, and many greens in general.

Ways to use:
If you're looking for the most adaptable component in this book, you've found it! Whether sweet or savory, it's hard to flip to a page in this book and not find an excuse to throw on a handful of basil.

— In sabzi khordan (page 70)
— As the base for tabbouleh (page 72)
— For larb gai (page 74)
— Add a giant handful to dressed greens (page 140)
— Make a pesto with any of these leafy herbs
— Find a recipe for kuku sabzi (a Persian egg dish with almost more herbs than eggs)

Sabzi khordan

If you're serving sabzi khordan to uninitiated guests (anyone lacking familiarity with Persian food), you will absolutely spend more time explaining it than actually making it. It takes literally one minute to throw some herbs on a plate with a block of feta and some pita, but it takes a lot longer to explain to your guests that, yes, you can (and should) eat an entire fistful of basil with your cheese and bread. Don't worry, they'll thank you later. This formula can be scaled up and down to serve 1 or 100 people!

⊘ **5+ MIN**
⊖ 15+ MIN
⊙ 30+ MIN

8 servings

Any combination of fresh cilantro, parsley, mint, basil, green onions, chives, or dill (about 3 bunches total)
One 8 oz [225 g] block of feta or extra-virgin olive oil, for drizzling
Marinated beets (page 29), sliced radishes, or tomatoes (all optional)
8 pitas or another soft flatbread

After washing and drying the herbs, remove any large stems and arrange the herbs on a plate (in a big pile with room to the side, or in a wreath with room in the center for the feta). Place the feta, marinated beets, radishes, or tomatoes on the plate, if using. If you're not using feta, drizzle the herbs with a little olive oil.

To eat, take a small piece of pita, place a little piece of feta on it, and pile on the herbs.

Tabbouleh

While the parsley/mint/green onion tabbouleh that I grew up with is a classic for a reason, I love getting creative with the mixture and subbing in other herbs. Feel free to do the same here, and use whatever combination of leafy herbs sounds good to you. Remember that there are a few crucial features of tabbouleh: 1) Everything must be finely chopped (no big pieces!). 2) Don't use "too much" bulgur. The exact meaning of "too much" is up for debate. Some folks add a teaspoon of bulgur, and some add a half cup. As a rule of thumb, remember that the herbs aren't just a seasoning—they're the backbone of this dish.

———————

⏱ 5+ MIN
◔ **15+ MIN**
⊙ 30+ MIN

4 to 6 servings

⅓ cup [70 g] fine bulgur #1, plus
   more as needed
2 cups [425 g] minced tomatoes,
   from about 3 medium
¼ cup [60 g] lemon juice
Salt
**2 cups [100 g] minced fresh
   parsley (from about 2 medium
   bunches)**
**1 cup [60 g] minced green onions
   (from about ½ of 1 small bunch)**
**1 cup [40 g] minced fresh basil
   leaves (from about 1 medium
   bunch)**
3 Tbsp extra-virgin olive oil
¼ tsp freshly ground black pepper

Combine the uncooked bulgur, tomatoes, lemon juice, and ¼ tsp salt in a medium mixing bowl. Stir together, and then smooth out so it's in one even layer. Allow to hydrate while you prep the rest of the ingredients. If it still looks very watery after about 10 minutes, add 2 to 3 Tbsp more bulgur, stir together, and let sit longer (tomatoes vary in juiciness).

Add the parsley, green onions, basil, olive oil, and pepper, and stir together to combine. Right before serving, sprinkle with a little more salt, to taste.

Recipe notes
Fine bulgur does not need to be cooked, just re-hydrated. If you want to use coarser bulgur, cook in boiling water until al dente, strain it well, move to a container, top with lemon juice while it's still hot, then add the tomatoes.

Substitutions
Use 1 cup [35 g] of minced fresh mint instead of basil for a more classic tabbouleh. Or use a combination of both, if you've got them on hand. If you don't have either, you can use extra parsley in place of the basil, along with 1 to 2 tsp dried mint (to taste). You can also replace all the parsley with 2 cups [100 g] fresh cilantro for a very different take.

Make-ahead instructions
Wash and store your herbs as on page 69. A day or two before, you can chop the parsley and green onions, and separately combine the tomato/lemon/bulgur mixture. Chop the basil (or mint) and throw everything together a few hours before serving, then salt it at the last minute. Leftovers will keep, refrigerated, for a couple days.

Larb gai

Larb gai was one of the first Thai dishes I fell in love with, and one of the meals I made all the time when I was first living on my own. It's made up of ingredients you can easily find in your average US supermarket, but it's so much more than the sum of its parts.

———————

⏱ 5+ MIN
◷ 15+ MIN
ⓘ **30+ MIN**

4 servings

1 head iceberg lettuce
2 Tbsp jasmine rice
¼ cup [60 g] water
1 lb [455 g] ground chicken
1 large shallot, very thinly sliced
1 Thai red chile, thinly sliced
   (optional)
3 Tbsp lime juice
1 to 2 Tbsp fish sauce
½ tsp chili powder
½ cup [20 g] chopped fresh cilantro
⅓ cup [10 g] packed fresh mint leaves
⅓ cup [15 g] thinly sliced green onions
Lime wedges, for serving

Cut the lettuce in half from stem to end, then in half again the same way to make quarters. Rinse under water, shake the quarters dry, and set aside. Cut the stem end off each quarter so the leaves can easily separate (but leave them whole).

Preheat a sauté pan over medium heat. Once hot, add the rice and cook, stirring constantly, for 7 to 10 minutes, until it's uniformly golden brown. Transfer the rice to a spice grinder or mortar and pestle and pulverize almost to a powder. It's OK if it's gritty, but there should be no chunks of rice. Set aside.

Place the water in the sauté pan and bring to a simmer over medium heat. As soon as it starts simmering, add the chicken. Break the chicken into small bits with a spoon as it cooks, stirring for about 5 minutes until cooked through (do not let it brown). Drain the excess liquid.

Add the shallot and sliced chile, if using, to the skillet and stir together, letting them soften a little for about 2 minutes while stirring constantly. Remove from the heat.

Add the lime juice, 1 Tbsp of the fish sauce, chili powder, and toasted rice powder to the cooled-down skillet, and toss everything together to coat evenly. Taste and sprinkle on a little more fish sauce, as needed.

Fold in the cilantro, mint, and green onions, and serve immediately with the iceberg lettuce for scooping and lime wedges on the side.

Make-ahead instructions
Make the chicken mixture ahead all the way through adding the lime sauce. Set aside in the fridge, and fold in the herbs at the last minute (either reheat before adding the herbs or serve cold). As the mixture sits, the flavors mellow a bit, so be sure to sprinkle with extra lime juice right before serving.

Other components you can use
You can make this recipe pescatarian (almost vegan) by replacing the sautéed chicken with a batch of garlicky mushrooms (page 77). Proceed with the recipe from there, and dress them as you would the chicken, reserving some sauce and tasting as you go.

Garlicky mushrooms

Mushrooms give off a ton of liquid as they cook, and it's up to you to make sure that liquid cooks off completely. This will take longer if you crowd the pan, but that's OK! Despite their name, mushrooms will never become mushy, even if you have to cook them for a really long time.

———————

Makes 2½ cups [325 g], enough to make all 3 recipes in this section

1½ lb [680 g] cremini mushrooms
3 Tbsp extra-virgin olive oil
½ tsp salt
1½ Tbsp pressed or minced garlic
(see recipe notes)

Brush the mushrooms clean with a paper towel, and cut them into ½ in [13 mm] wedges or slice them thinly.

Place the mushrooms, olive oil, and salt in a large sauté pan and set over medium-high heat. Once it starts to sizzle rapidly, cook for 10 to 12 minutes, stirring occasionally, until the liquid the mushrooms give off evaporates. Lower the heat to medium and continue to cook, stirring frequently, just until they brown, about 5 more minutes.

Lower the heat to low and add the garlic. Stir constantly until the garlic smells toasty (but not burnt), about 2 more minutes. Remove from the heat.

Recipe notes
You don't need to worry about crowding the pan, but the less wide your pan is, the longer it will take for the liquid to cook off. So if you double this recipe or use a small pan, you might be better off working in 2 batches.

Use whatever mushrooms you'd like here (for instance, sliced shiitake, or even button mushrooms cut into wedges), but note that some varieties will lose much more moisture and will take less time to sear, so start with more than you think you'll need just in case.

You can increase to 2 or even 3 Tbsp of garlic if you're a huge garlic fan or if you want to use these in a recipe where you want the garlic flavor to dominate.

Storage
Garlicky mushrooms will keep for up to 5 days in the refrigerator, and for at least 3 months tightly sealed in the freezer with no loss of quality.

Ways to use:
— In a mushroom omelette (page 78)
— For garlicky mushroom chestnut soup (page 80)
— Atop a pizza bianca ai funghi (page 82)
— Top the cornmeal pancake stack on page 106 in place of the slow-roasted tomatoes
— Layer into the summer strata on page 104 in place of some of the other veggies
— Use in place of eggplant in the Chicago-style deep-dish pizza recipe on page 58
— Replace the sautéed chicken in the larb gai on page 74
— Change up the tacos on page 114 by replacing the shrimp with these mushrooms and add a little Cotija cheese to make them vegetarian
— Add a handful to a grain bowl or to spaghetti aglio e olio (page 66)
— Add to your favorite soup or stew for some extra-savory flavor

Mushroom omelette

French and American omelettes feel emblematic of their respective cuisines. French omelettes are restrained yet indulgent, while American omelettes are delivery devices for bold flavors. And since this book loves a flavor-delivery device, it's probably no surprise that our omelette of choice here is American.

⏱ **5+ MIN**
⊝ 15+ MIN
ⓘ 30+ MIN

2 to 4 servings

6 large eggs
2 Tbsp unsalted butter
½ tsp salt
¾ cup [95 g] garlicky mushrooms (page 77)
2 Tbsp minced fresh chives (optional)

Break the eggs into a small mixing bowl and beat together until you no longer see clear flecks of white.

Place 1 Tbsp of the butter in a nonstick pan and place over medium-high heat. When the butter is sizzling rapidly, add half of the eggs and ¼ tsp of the salt. Slowly agitate the eggs with a silicone spatula. Stop agitating once they're runny with some large curds (about 30 seconds). Sprinkle half of the mushrooms and ½ Tbsp of the chives, if using, over one side, and let sit for about 10 seconds.

Use your spatula to fold the bare half over the mushroom half. Cook for 30 more seconds on one side, then flip and cook for 30 more seconds on the other side.

Transfer the omelette to a plate, sprinkle on another ½ Tbsp of the chives, and serve immediately. Repeat with the remaining ingredients to make the second omelette.

Substitutions
Replace the chives with basil, cilantro, or parsley. Include a handful of fresh spinach, fresh tomatoes, and/or your favorite cheese with the mushrooms.

Other components you can use
Caramelized tomatoes (page 101), jammy onions (page 85), grilled corn (page 45), and smoky eggplant (page 53) work great as an omelette filling. Gochujang sauce (page 181) is great for drizzling on top.

Garlicky mushroom chestnut soup

When you've got garlicky mushrooms on hand in the fridge or freezer, garlicky mushroom chestnut soup comes together surprisingly quickly. Chestnuts make for an exceptionally creamy soup, which is the perfect base to carry all that garlicky mushroom flavor.

⊘ 5+ MIN
⊖ **15+ MIN**
ⓘ 30+ MIN

4 servings

3 Tbsp unsalted butter
1 medium onion, diced or thinly
  sliced
Salt
**1 cup [130 g] garlicky mushrooms
  (page 77), plus ⅔ cup [85 g] for
  garnish (optional)**
40 roasted peeled chestnuts
3 cups [705 g] chicken stock, plus
  more as needed
1 tsp dried rubbed sage
¼ tsp freshly ground black pepper
Sour cream, for garnish (optional)
Fresh chives or parsley, for garnish
  (optional)

Melt the butter in a stockpot over medium heat. Add the onion and a pinch of salt. Cook, stirring occasionally, for about 8 minutes, just until it softens.

Add 1 cup [130 g] of the mushrooms, the chestnuts, chicken stock, sage, and pepper and increase the heat to high. Once the soup comes to a boil, lower the heat to medium-high and let it simmer gently for about 10 minutes, just to allow the flavors to meld.

Purée completely with an immersion blender (or in a standing blender). Taste and adjust the seasoning if necessary. If it's too thick, thin it out with a touch more stock or water.

Spoon into bowls and top each with a spoonful of the remaining mushrooms, if using. Add a dollop of sour cream and a sprinkling of chives, if using.

Recipe notes
This recipe is creamy and flavorful without the sour cream, so you can easily omit it, substitute a vegan butter, and use vegetable stock to make it vegan. Also, feel free to use packets of ready-roasted or steamed chestnuts (you want 11.3 oz [320 g] of peeled chestnuts). If you're not making the component ahead of time, you can sauté 16 oz [455 g] of mushrooms in the pot you plan to cook the soup in, remove them, and proceed with the recipe without washing the pot.

Make-ahead instructions
The soup can be made a day ahead and then reheated on the stove or microwave. Set it over low heat, add a little water, and stir occasionally. You can also freeze it for about 3 months—thaw in the fridge the day before and reheat in the microwave.

Pizza bianca ai funghi

This pizza bianca is inspired by Joe Beddia (of Pizzeria Beddia) and his famous white pie, which is slathered in what's essentially a savory whipped cream. During a quick 5-minute bake on a hot stone, the crust puffs, the cheese blisters, and the white sauce holds it all together while remaining creamy and melting just a tad.

⊘ 5+ MIN
⊖ 15+ MIN
① **30+ MIN**

**4 appetizer servings or
2 main servings**

¾ cup [175 g] room-temperature
  water
1 tsp active dry yeast
2 cups [260 g] all-purpose flour,
  plus more for dusting
½ tsp salt
½ cup [115 g] heavy whipping
  cream
1 Tbsp lemon juice
1 Tbsp pressed or minced garlic
¼ tsp lemon zest
¼ tsp freshly ground black pepper
Sea salt
Cornmeal, for sprinkling
1½ cups [150 g] shredded
  mozzarella
**¾ cup [100 g] garlicky mushrooms
  (page 77)**
1 handful fresh basil leaves

Place the water and yeast in the bowl of a stand mixer fitted with the hook attachment. Stir together until the yeast dissolves. Add the flour and salt and mix on low speed to bring everything together. Increase the speed to medium and knead for about 5 minutes, until the dough smooths out.

Remove the dough from the dough hook, place it back in the bowl, cover loosely, and let it rise for about 1½ hours in a warm spot in your kitchen. It's done rising once it's doubled in size.

When your dough is almost done rising, prep your toppings: Place the whipping cream, lemon juice, garlic, lemon zest, pepper, and a small pinch of sea salt in the bowl of a stand mixer fitted with the whisk. Beat to stiff peaks.

Lightly flour a clean counter. Divide the dough in half and shape each half into a ball. Roll one ball out to about ⅛ to ¼ in [3 to 6 mm] thick. Place on a cutting board that's been generously sprinkled with cornmeal. Spread half of the whipped cream mixture over the dough, then top with about half of the mozzarella and half of the mushrooms. Repeat with the other ball. Let them rest for 10 to 20 minutes while you preheat your oven.

Place a pizza stone or sheet pan directly on the floor of your oven (not on a rack), and preheat the oven to 500°F [260°C].

Slide one pizza onto the hot stone. Bake for about 5 minutes, until the pizza is bubbly and golden brown in spots. Top with basil at the table. Repeat with the second pizza.

Recipe note
To grill, lightly oil your gas grill's grates, then preheat it to its highest setting with the lid closed. Once your grill has heated for several minutes, slide the pizzas off the cutting boards onto the grates and immediately shut the lid. Grill for about 5 minutes, just until the dough is cooked through and the cheese is bubbling. Rotate exactly one time halfway through to make sure they're cooking evenly.

Make-ahead instructions
You can make the dough a few days ahead of time, let it rise at room temperature for about 1 hour, then store it, covered, in the fridge. Prep the whipped cream up to 3 days ahead.

Substitutions
You can use 1 lb [455 g] of store-bought pizza dough to make this recipe even easier.

Other components you can use
Use a total of ⅓ cup [75 g] toum (divided between the 2 pies) instead of the entire whipped cream mixture. Or use toum and sub vegan shredded cheese to make it vegan. Try replacing some or all of the mushrooms with smoky eggplant (page 53), jammy onions (page 85), or grilled corn (page 45).

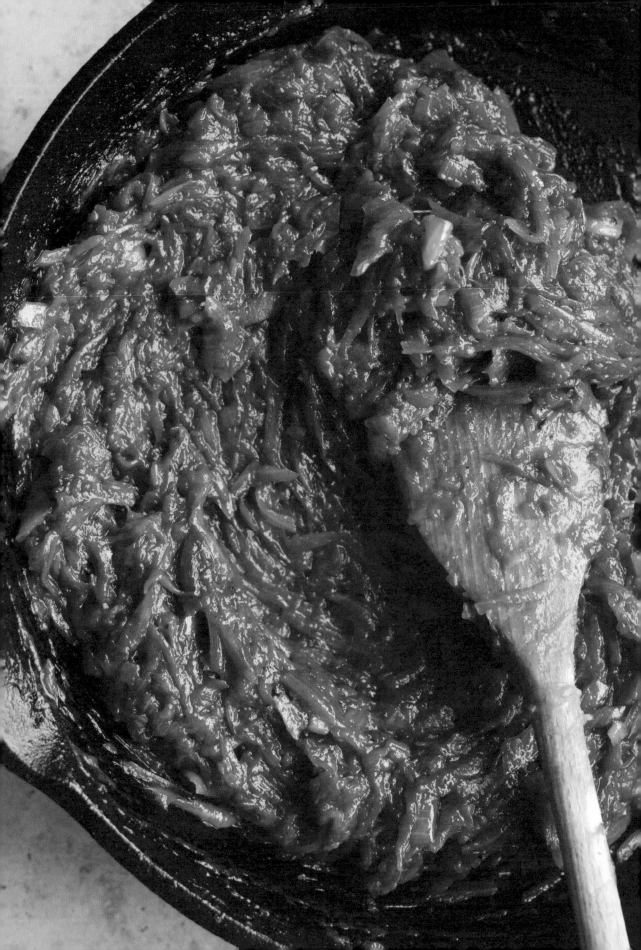

Jammy onions

When I say jammy, I mean jammy. This technique doesn't just yield lightly charred onion slices—it results in deeply sweet, dark brown, spreadably soft caramelized onions. If you're a fan of French onion soup, keep these in the freezer so you can whip up a batch anytime, or use them to add a heavy dose of caramelized onion flavor to all your favorite dishes. Since it's best made in smaller batches, one batch of jammy onions is exactly enough to make either mujadara or French onion soup, or more than enough for a batch of chutney.

Makes 2½ cups [630 g], enough to make any 1 recipe from this section

¼ cup [55 g] extra-virgin olive oil
7 medium or 5 large onions, sliced
1 tsp salt

Place the olive oil, onions, salt, and about 2 Tbsp of water in a wide sauté pan or large Dutch oven over medium-high heat. Stir together. Once they start sizzling, cover and let them cook until softened and a brown film has developed on the bottom of the pan, 5 to 10 minutes. Uncover and scrape up the film, incorporating it into the onion mixture. Add 1 Tbsp more of water if it is stubborn.

Continue cooking, uncovered, for about 35 minutes, scraping the bottom of the pan every time a brown film develops, and deglazing with 1 Tbsp of water if needed to loosen. Adjust the heat so you are stirring and scraping every 2 to 3 minutes. You'll need to deglaze and stir more frequently toward the end, and will need to lower the heat gradually.

When the onion mixture has shrunk to about one quarter of its original volume and turned deeply golden brown, it's done.

Recipe notes
This recipe is all about the real estate the onions have to cook on. If you double this recipe, it will take longer for the onions to cook down and you will need to use a larger pot. The wider the pot or pan, the less time they will take to cook. If you halve the recipe, they will take less time to cook down.

Storage
Jammy onions will last in the fridge for about 4 days, or tightly sealed in the freezer for at least 3 months with no loss of quality.

Store-bought alternatives
While you can't use anything store-bought to make French onion soup or mujadara, you can use a store-bought caramelized onion chutney to top a steak, or buy Vietnamese crispy fried shallots to add some oniony crunch to a salad or pasta.

Ways to use:
— Atop grilled steak (page 86)
— For easiest French onion soup (page 88)
— In mujadara (page 90)
— Use in place of mushrooms on the pizza bianca on page 82
— Replace some of the eggplant in the Chicago-style deep-dish pizza on page 58
— Tuck into an omelette (see page 78)
— Make a charcuterie board with jammy onions, Gruyère cheese, store-bought pâté, red grapes, and a few sprigs fresh thyme or rosemary
— Add to your favorite sandwich

Grilled steak with jammy onion chutney

This caramelized onion chutney takes literally 3 minutes to come together when you're starting with jammy onions. If you're not a big meat eater, it's also lovely in a grilled cheese sandwich or in a grain bowl.

_____

⊘ **5+ MIN**
⊖ 15+ MIN
ⓘ 30+ MIN

4 servings

1 cup [250 g] jammy onions
  (page 85)
¼ cup [60 g] balsamic vinegar
3 Tbsp brown sugar
1 tsp Dijon mustard
¼ tsp dried thyme
Freshly ground black pepper
4 New York strip steaks
  (2¼ lb [1 kg] total)
Salt

Place the jammy onions in a wide sauté pan. Top with the vinegar, brown sugar, mustard, thyme, and ¼ tsp pepper. Stir together and bring to a simmer over medium-high heat. Lower the heat to medium or medium-low to maintain a simmer for about 2 minutes, just until it thickens. Remove from the heat, transfer to a container, let cool for about 30 minutes at room temperature, then transfer to the fridge to chill.

To grill or sear the steaks, sprinkle the steaks with slightly more than ½ tsp salt per 1 lb of meat (or divide the steaks' weight in grams by 140, and use that many grams of salt), and a few grinds of pepper. Let them sit at room temperature for about 15 minutes. Lightly oil the grill grates and preheat the grill to high. Once it's heated, place the steaks on the grill and sear for 3 to 4 minutes on each side, until medium-rare (130°F [55°C]).

Place the steaks on a serving plate, top with the chutney, and serve immediately.

Make-ahead instructions
The chutney keeps in the fridge for at least a week, but you can also freeze it for months. Make the chutney and salt the steaks a day or two before you plan to sear them, store them separately in the fridge, and sear the steaks at the last minute.

Other components you can use
Steak is also wonderful topped with caramelized tomatoes (page 101), garlicky mushrooms (page 77), cilantro lime dressing (page 147), pickled mango (page 227), or gochujang sauce (page 181).

Easiest French onion soup

⏱ 5+ MIN
◐ **15+ MIN**
◷ 30+ MIN

6 servings

1 loaf crusty bread, sliced ¾ in [2 cm] thick

10 oz [285 g] Swiss (such as Jarlsberg or Gruyère), grated or sliced

1 batch jammy onions (page 85)

2 Tbsp all-purpose flour

2 qt [1.9 L] chicken or vegetable stock

½ cup [115 g] dry red wine

1 Tbsp red wine vinegar

½ tsp dried thyme

½ tsp dried rubbed sage

Pinch of sugar

Since this recipe is incredibly simple, it's important to use a good quality stock, whether store-bought or homemade. If your stock is not particularly delicious, add a little dried sage, thyme, and black pepper, as needed, and it'll turn out great.

————

Preheat your broiler. Place 6 bread slices on a parchment-lined sheet pan. Broil until toasted on one side (1 to 5 minutes, depending on your broiler). Flip the slices over and place the cheese on the untoasted side. Place back under the broiler and toast until the cheese is melted and browned in spots (another 1 to 5 minutes). Set aside.

Place the jammy onions in a stockpot off the heat, add the flour, and stir together until there are no lumps. Add the stock, wine, vinegar, herbs, and sugar and stir together. Bring to a simmer over medium-high heat. Lower the heat to low and let it simmer until the flavors meld, 5 to 10 minutes. Taste and adjust the seasoning as needed. Serve in bowls topped with the cheesy toasts.

Make-ahead instructions
Store the soup in the fridge for up to 4 days or in the freezer for at least 3 months, and store the cheesy toasts in the freezer for up to 2 months (reheat in the toaster oven until thawed and crisp).

Mujadara

This book is all about flavor-packed components breathing life into humble ingredients, and mujadara is perhaps the most iconic example of this idea. Lentils and rice on their own are just fine. But take seven onions, cook them down to almost nothing, fry most until chewy-crisp, fold into a perfectly cooked pot of lentils and rice, and enjoy every flavor-infused bite.

———

⏱ 5+ MIN
◔ 15+ MIN
ⓘ **30+ MIN**

8 servings

For the lentils and rice:
1 lb [455 g] green or brown lentils, sorted and rinsed
⅓ **batch jammy onions (page 85)**
1¼ cups [250 g] basmati rice, rinsed
1½ tsp salt
2⅔ cups [625 g] water, plus more to cook the lentils

For the fried onions:
High-smoke-point neutral oil, for frying (such as canola)
⅔ **batch jammy onions (page 85)**

To make the lentils and rice, cover the lentils with a few inches of water in a small stockpot or Dutch oven and bring to a boil over high heat. Lower the heat to medium to maintain a low boil, and cook for about 10 minutes. They're done once they're unpleasantly al dente, not soft. You should be able to chew one, but it will be gritty.

Strain and rinse your par-cooked lentils and wipe any scum from the edge of the pot. Return the lentils to the pot and add the jammy onions, rinsed rice, salt to taste, and water. Stir together, smooth into an even layer, and set over medium-high heat. Once it starts simmering, cover and gradually lower the heat to low in the first couple minutes. Let it simmer, covered, for 15 minutes, then let it rest for 15 minutes. Do not peek, even once it's done cooking.

While your lentils cook, make the fried onions. Heat ½ in [13 mm] of oil in a sauté pan over medium-high heat for a few minutes. It's hot enough once an onion dropped in the oil starts to sizzle immediately. Cook the onions in 3 batches: Add one-third of the onions to the oil and agitate them so they don't all stick together. Let them cook for about 5 minutes, then remove with a slotted spoon once they are very deeply browned and crunchy but not burnt. Repeat with the remaining onions.

Once the lentils and rice are done, stir in half of the onions, then top with more and serve.

Make-ahead instructions
Mujadara is best made at the last moment, but leftovers will keep for several days in the fridge. If you're serving this for guests, you can fry the onions, then boil and rinse the lentils and return them to the pot. Refrigerate the container of fried onions, the container of jammy onions, and the pot of lentils, then proceed when guests arrive. The lentils and rice can rest off the heat for up to 45 minutes without removing the lid.

Other components you can use
While there's no substitute for the jammy onions here, mujadara goes nicely with the tzatziki on page 199.

Miso sweet potatoes

Miso can be a beautifully subtle ingredient, but when I want it to pack a punch, I do one simple thing: I use miso like it's salt, and I leave the plain old salt behind. By skipping the salt, I don't have to hold back on the miso at all. Here, sweet potatoes are coated in as much miso butter as possible, until they're perfectly seasoned and absurdly flavorful. If you double or triple this recipe to make multiple recipes with it, make sure you use multiple sheet pans (avoid crowding your pans).

———

Makes 3 cups whole or 1½ cups [370 g] puréed, enough to make any 1 recipe from this section

2 medium sweet potatoes
¼ cup [70 g] red miso paste
1 Tbsp honey
1 Tbsp butter, melted

Preheat the oven to 450°F [230°C] and line a sheet pan with parchment paper.

Slice the sweet potatoes into ½ in [13 mm] wedges and place on the sheet pan in a single layer.

In a small bowl, mix together the miso, honey, and melted butter until smooth. Brush the mixture on one side of the sweet potatoes in a thick layer, then flip and brush the other side.

Bake for 15 minutes, until caramelized and tender. To purée (optional), smash with the back of a fork until smooth.

Storage
Miso sweet potatoes will keep in the fridge for 4 to 5 days, or the freezer for up to 3 months in a tightly sealed container. Since they're not supposed to be crispy, you can reheat or thaw them in the microwave with no issues.

Ways to use:
— Top with sesame seeds, lime juice, and green onions (page 94)
— Use in sweet potato broccoli grain bowls (page 96)
— Bake into miso sweet potato caramel brownies (page 98)
— Make the bibimbap on page 186 vegetarian by using miso sweet potato bites instead of beef
— Replace some of the veggies in the cold soba noodles on page 194 with miso sweet potatoes
— Find a recipe for roasted sweet potato pie and use these miso sweet potatoes for a savory twist
— Throw into a salad that needs some umami, creaminess, and sweetness

Miso sweet potatoes with sesame and lime

Miso sweet potatoes work great as a side on their own, but if you want something that's 100% fancier and only like 1% more effort, serve them with lime wedges, a sprinkling of sesame seeds, and thinly sliced green onions.

———————

⏱ **5+ MIN**
⊖ 15+ MIN
◔ 30+ MIN

4 servings

1 batch miso sweet potatoes (page 93)
4 lime wedges
⅓ cup [20 g] thinly sliced green onions
Sesame seeds, for garnish

Place the roasted sweet potatoes in a serving bowl, place lime wedges to the side, and top with the green onions and sesame seeds to taste.

Sweet potato broccoli grain bowls

Grain bowls are transformative: Take a bunch of random vegetables from your fridge or freezer, throw them over brown rice, drizzle on a delicious sauce, and you're set. Or do something slightly more intentional and carefully prepare and layer together your favorite ingredients. Whether intentional or slapdash, it's going to be good. Use this recipe as a jumping-off point, sub in your other favorite vegetables, and drizzle on some salsa verde (page 163) or cilantro lime dressing (page 147) if they suit your ingredients better than sesame ginger sauce.

⊘ 5+ MIN
⊖ **15+ MIN**
① 30+ MIN

4 servings

Salt
1⅓ cups [240 g] brown rice
1 crown broccoli
1 Tbsp soy sauce
1 Tbsp rice vinegar
1 Tbsp water
1 Tbsp brown sugar
1 Tbsp sesame oil
3 cups [200 g] thinly shredded
   red cabbage
1 batch miso sweet potatoes
   (page 93)
One 15 oz [425 g] can chickpeas,
   drained and rinsed
½ cup [70 g] crumbled feta
1 batch sesame ginger sauce
   (page 191)

Place a stockpot of lightly salted water over high heat and bring to a boil. Once boiling, add the brown rice and cook until done (times vary, so follow the timing on the package).

While the rice is cooking, prep the broccoli. Cut the broccoli into small florets and set aside. In a small bowl, whisk together the soy sauce, vinegar, water, and brown sugar until the sugar dissolves. Set aside. Heat a sauté pan over medium-high heat. Add the sesame oil, swirl, and immediately add the broccoli. Toss for about 5 minutes, until al dente, bright green, and browned in spots. Lower the heat to medium-low and pour the soy sauce mixture evenly over the broccoli. Immediately toss together for about 1 minute, until excess moisture cooks off and the thickened sauce clings to the broccoli. Set aside.

As soon as the rice is done, add the cabbage to the pot with the rice and cook for 30 to 60 seconds. Drain, taste, adjust the seasoning as necessary, and divide among 4 bowls.

Top each bowl with sweet potatoes, broccoli, chickpeas, and feta. Right before serving, top with some of the sesame ginger sauce to taste.

Make-ahead instructions
You can make the individual components 2 to 3 days ahead of time, then assemble as needed.

Other components you can mix and match
Caramelized tomatoes (page 101), garlicky mushrooms (page 77), grilled corn (page 45), leafy herbs (page 69), marinated beets (page 29), coconut shrimp (page 111), lemongrass beef (page 127), or za'atar cauliflower (page 37). Use your favorite sauce if you're changing up the flavors dramatically (the cilantro lime dressing on page 147 goes with almost anything).

Miso sweet potato caramel brownies

I know exactly what you're thinking: These brownies better not contain carob or flaxseed. I hate to disappoint all the carob stans out there, but for everyone else: I assure you, these brownies are quite conventional. Sweet potatoes add a fudgy chewiness, and miso adds a salty umami note to complement the chocolate and caramel.

———————

⏱ 5+ MIN
◔ 15+ MIN
ⓘ **30+ MIN**

16 brownies

For the miso caramel:
½ cup [115 g] heavy cream
2 Tbsp red miso paste
6 Tbsp [85 g] unsalted butter,
   cut into small pieces
1 cup [200 g] sugar

For the brownies:
Butter, for greasing the pan
1 cup [130 g] all-purpose flour
½ cup [40 g] cocoa powder
½ tsp baking powder
¼ tsp salt
1⅔ cups [335 g] sugar
**1 cup [245 g] puréed miso sweet
   potatoes (page 93)**
½ cup [105 g] canola oil
1 large egg

To make the miso caramel, stir together the cream and miso in a liquid measuring cup until the miso is broken up. Place the butter in the measuring cup and set the cup within arm's reach of the stove. Also have a whisk handy.

Place the sugar in a medium saucepan and set over medium-high heat. Let it heat for about 3 minutes, until the edges and bottom start to melt and turn light amber. At this point, lower the heat to medium and begin stirring it constantly with a heatproof spatula. Once the sugar becomes a runny amber liquid (about 4 minutes after the edges start to melt), lower the heat to low and continue to cook for 1 to 2 more minutes while stirring constantly until it's completely lump-free, a little darker, and smells caramelly (see recipe note).

Carefully add the cream mixture and whisk until completely smooth. Remove from the heat, pour the caramel into another container, and let cool to room temperature before using.

To make the brownies, preheat the oven to 350°F [180°C]. Butter an 8 by 8 in [20 by 20 cm] nonstick pan and line the bottom with parchment.

Sift together the flour, cocoa, baking powder, and salt in a medium mixing bowl. In another mixing bowl, slowly whisk together the sugar, puréed sweet potatoes, canola oil, and egg (do not incorporate air). Pour the wet ingredients over the dry ingredients and stir together just enough to combine (do not overmix).

Pour the mixture into the prepared pan, smooth out the top, and bake for about 40 minutes, until a toothpick inserted into the center comes out clean.

Let the brownies cool in the pan for about 10 minutes, then trace around the edge with a knife. Invert the brownies out of the pan, then invert again onto a serving plate. Chill for 30 minutes, top with half of the caramel sauce, and chill again for 1 hour longer before slicing. Serve with more caramel at the table.

Recipe note
The time it takes for your sugar to caramelize will vary, so pay attention to sight and smell cues, and use your own judgment to make sure it doesn't burn.

Make-ahead instructions
The caramel will last in the fridge for a couple weeks. You can store the brownies (caramel and all) in the fridge for several days, but they'll last for at least 3 months in the freezer with no loss of quality.

Caramelized tomatoes

These caramelized tomatoes inspired the idea for this book. They're like the shortstop of your freezer, and they will save dinner no matter what you throw at them. So try to keep them on hand, and always make extra if you can.

———————

Makes 2¾ cups [670 g], enough to make all 3 recipes in this section

14 tomatoes
1½ Tbsp extra-virgin olive oil
4 garlic cloves, crushed through a press
½ tsp salt

Preheat the oven to 350°F [180°C].

Carefully pull any vines or stems off your tomatoes, but do not hull them. Slice the tomatoes in half across their equators. Place on a rimmed sheet pan, drizzle with the olive oil, and use your hands to coat evenly. Flip the tomatoes so they are all cut-side up on the sheet pan and spaced out evenly. Evenly sprinkle with the garlic and salt.

Roast for about 2½ hours (longer for larger tomatoes, shorter for smaller ones). If your oven has a tight seal, open the door a few times while they cook to let the steam escape. They will shrink down significantly, and they should be syrupy, not dry, and caramelized in spots around their edges.

Recipe note
You can make this recipe with cherry tomatoes. If you'd like to make all three recipes in the section, you'll need 7 pints [2.1 kg] of cherry tomatoes, and you will need to use two sheet pans. Whether you make the full amount or a smaller amount, cherry tomatoes will take less time (about 1 hour).

Storage
Caramelized tomatoes will keep in the fridge for up to 5 days. But they will keep for at least 3 months in the freezer in a tightly sealed container with no loss of quality, so freeze whatever you don't plan to use right away.

Freeze in a single layer on a flexible cutting board, then transfer to a resealable bag, squeeze out as much air as you can, and store in the freezer.

Thaw as needed by placing them in the fridge overnight, or microwave tomatoes at low wattage until thawed.

Easier alternatives
This section's caramelized caprese and cornmeal pancake stack both work great with marinated fresh tomatoes. Just cut your tomatoes into big slices, drizzle with a little bit of red wine vinegar, olive oil, salt, basil and/or oregano (either fresh or dried), and some crushed garlic. Mix together and let sit for about 30 minutes, then strain out of the liquid to use.

Ways to use:
— For caramelized caprese (page 102)
— Atop a cornmeal pancake stack (page 106) with black beans, goat cheese, and greens
— In summer strata (page 104) with dressed greens
— Make the most umami PLT (page 176) ever by replacing fresh tomatoes with a smaller amount of caramelized tomatoes
— Layer in a few pieces in place of the fresh tomatoes in the eggplant ricotta frittata on page 56
— Tuck into an omelette (page 78)
— Add to a grain bowl with cilantro lime dressing (page 147).
— Cut with kitchen shears right on the sheet pan after roasting and mash with a fork to turn into an incredibly flavorful roasted tomato sauce
— Toast an everything bagel, top with cream cheese, and smash on a caramelized tomato half
— Make the best English breakfast ever: sunny-side-up eggs, breakfast sausages, toast, and one caramelized tomato half per person

Caramelized caprese

While it's not prohibitively expensive to buy a small bunch of hydroponically grown basil in the middle of winter, you'll be hard-pressed to find a deal on quality tomatoes outside late summer. But this caprese is there for you, no matter the time of year, as long as you've got caramelized tomatoes in your freezer. Or even if you don't, slow-roasting is the best way to turn mediocre out-of-season tomatoes into delicious little gems.

———

5+ MIN
15+ MIN
30+ MIN

4 servings as an appetizer

8 oz [225 g] fresh buffalo
 mozzarella
**6 caramelized tomato halves
 (page 101)**
1 small bunch fresh basil
Extra-virgin olive oil, for drizzling
Balsamic vinegar, for drizzling
Sea salt (optional)

Slice the buffalo mozzarella into pieces about the size of your caramelized tomatoes. Tear the basil leaves from the bunch, then wash and dry them. Layer the mozzarella, tomato, and basil together on a plate. Drizzle lightly with olive oil and balsamic vinegar, and sprinkle with sea salt, if using (but keep in mind that the tomatoes are already moderately seasoned).

Substitutions
Try layering in a few marinated beets (page 29) in place of some of the tomatoes.

Summer strata

This strata is ideal for taking advantage of summer produce, but you can truly make it any time of the year, especially if you had the foresight to freeze a stash of caramelized tomatoes in the late summer.

⏱ 5+ MIN
⊖ **15+ MIN**
ⓘ 30+ MIN

6 servings

Extra-virgin olive oil, for greasing
    the pan
6 cups [250 g] crusty bread cubes,
    cut ¾ in [2 cm]
¾ cup [180 g] whole milk
¼ cup [60 g] heavy cream
8 large eggs
4 to 6 garlic cloves, crushed
    through a press
1 tsp salt
¼ tsp freshly ground black pepper
8 oz [225 g] frozen spinach, thawed
    and wrung out very well
**12 caramelized tomato halves
    (page 101)**
2 cups [220 g] grated Cheddar
1 cup [140 g] corn kernels

Preheat the oven to 325°F [165°C].

Grease a 10 in [25 cm] cast-iron skillet or similar sized oven-proof casserole dish with oil. Place the bread in the skillet and bake for about 25 minutes, until dried out and a little golden. Remove from the oven and increase the temperature to 375°F [190°C].

Meanwhile, prep the rest of the filling. In a medium mixing bowl, whisk together the whole milk, cream, eggs, garlic, salt, and pepper, and set aside.

Place the spinach, most of the tomatoes, most of the Cheddar, and most of the corn in a large mixing bowl. Add the bread cubes and toss gently to distribute. Transfer the mixture to the skillet, sprinkle with the rest of the cheese, corn, and tomatoes, and pour the liquid ingredients evenly over everything. Let sit for 5 minutes, then bake for about 50 minutes, until puffy and cooked through.

Make-ahead instructions
The whole thing can be assembled the night before, refrigerated overnight, and then baked the next day (as long as you use something ovenproof besides cast-iron). Leave it on the counter for about 30 minutes before baking.

Other components you can use
Stick with the spinach and corn, which go with just about anything (and are probably already in your freezer). In place of the tomato, try the garlicky mushrooms (page 77). And if you're feeling ambitious, try grilling your corn for some extra smokiness (see page 45).

Cornmeal pancake stack

I'm not quite sure if this pancake stack qualifies as breakfast or dinner. But no matter the time of day you bring this to the table, no one's going to ask any questions.

⏱ 5+ MIN
◔ 15+ MIN
ⓘ **30+ MIN**

5 servings as a main or 10 as a side

For the kale:
1 tsp extra-virgin olive oil
Leaves from 1 medium bunch kale
Salt

For the pancakes and toppings:
1 cup [130 g] all-purpose flour
¾ cup [120 g] cornmeal
2 tsp baking powder
1 tsp salt
¼ tsp baking soda
2 cups [480 g] buttermilk
2 large eggs
3 Tbsp unsalted butter, melted, plus more cold butter for greasing the pan
2 Tbsp sugar
One 15 oz [425 g] can black beans, drained
10 caramelized tomato halves (page 101)
4 oz [115 g] chèvre

To make the kale, place a nonstick pan over medium heat for a few minutes. Add the oil, the kale, and a big pinch of salt. Toss around for about 4 minutes, until wilted down. Transfer the kale to a bowl and set aside. Remove the pan from the heat and wipe it out.

To make the pancakes, in a medium mixing bowl, whisk together the flour, cornmeal, baking powder, salt, and baking soda. In another mixing bowl, whisk together the buttermilk, eggs, melted butter, and sugar.

Place the nonstick pan back over medium heat for a few minutes. Once it's hot enough for a drop of water to sizzle off in about 10 seconds, mix up the batter by pouring the wet ingredients over the dry and stirring to combine. Stop mixing as soon as it smooths out.

Swipe the cold butter across the surface of the pan, then drop ¼ cup scoops of batter onto the pan. Once lots of bubbles break the surface and their craters do not disappear (2 to 3 minutes), flip and cook for 2 to 3 more minutes. Repeat with the remaining batter.

Serve about 3 pancakes per main serving with a heap of kale, the beans, tomato halves, and chèvre.

Recipe note
For a buttermilk substitute, do not use milk and lemon. Instead, use 1 cup [240 g] plain yogurt mixed with 1 cup [240 g] milk.

Make-ahead instructions
The cornmeal cakes can be made ahead and stored in the refrigerator for a couple days, or the freezer for at least 3 months. They will stale more quickly in the refrigerator. Reheat pancakes by throwing in the toaster on medium-low heat.

Kale can be sautéed a couple days ahead, or sautéed and frozen for at least 3 months.

Substitutions
See the fresh tomato substitution suggestion on page 101.

Other components you can use
These are also great with garlicky mushrooms (page 77) and/or grilled corn (page 45). Or try replacing the kale with za'atar cauliflower (page 37).

Meats

I should probably start off this, the littlest section, by confessing that I used to be a vegetarian. And while some meat lovers become vegetarian at great personal sacrifice, I have to admit, I was mostly a vegetarian because it was easy. You see, I simply did not enjoy eating meat. I love vegetables, I love carbs, and I'm a little keen on fruit. But meat? I didn't get the appeal, especially as the focal point of a meal.

But everything changed when I moved to Hong Kong years ago. Ironically, my love of carbs and vegetables was exactly what made it difficult to be a strict vegetarian in Hong Kong. The thing is, all of my favorite Chinese dishes take a tiny amount of super flavorful meat and cook it along with a larger amount of vegetables and carbs.

Take Sichuan dry-fried green beans or mapo tofu: Both dishes get so much flavor from a small amount of crispy browned bits of pork. Or lo mai gai, in which sticky rice gets its flavor not only from the lotus leaf it's wrapped in, but also from little bits of chicken and Chinese sausage.

Even now that I've moved away, I eat meat almost every day, but I do eat less meat than the average omnivore. I tend to use meat more as a flavoring and less as the main substance of a dish, but you'll find a bit of both in this section.

Coconut shrimp

This recipe is even sweeter and more coconutty than your average coconut shrimp recipe. Instead of egg, you dredge the shrimp in a flour-honey paste, then coat them in coconut and bread crumbs. This results in a slightly more delicate crust (so flip carefully), but they're so worth it.

___

Makes 25 to 45 shrimp (depending on size), enough to make any 1 recipe from this section

1 lb [455 g] raw, peeled shrimp
½ tsp salt
Freshly ground black pepper
3 Tbsp honey
⅓ cup [45 g] all-purpose flour, plus more as needed
1 cup [80 g] shredded coconut (see recipe note)
⅔ cup [45 g] panko bread crumbs
Coconut oil, for frying

Recipe note
You can substitute 2 cups [80 g] coconut flakes (the giant coconut shreds) for the shredded coconut—pulse them in a food processor a few times to break them up into small bits that are about the size of panko bread crumbs, or chop finely.

Storage
Store shrimp in a paper towel–lined container in the refrigerator after they cool completely (3 to 4 days). Reheat in a 375°F [190°C] oven (or toaster oven) for about 5 minutes, until crispy and warmed through. You can also freeze them and reheat in a 375°F [190°C] oven for about 8 minutes.

Place the shrimp in a mixing bowl and pat dry with paper towels. Sprinkle with the salt and a few grinds of pepper. Toss together to coat evenly. Drizzle with the honey, sprinkle with the flour, and toss to coat evenly (it should form a sticky paste—if it is runny, add a little more flour).

Place the shredded coconut and bread crumbs in another bowl, mix together, and set next to the shrimp bowl. Place an empty plate next to the coconut mixture.

Lift a few batter-coated shrimp out of the bowl and place in the coconut mixture. Toss around until evenly coated. Move to the empty plate to rest.

Line another plate with paper towels and place near the stove.

Set a sauté pan over medium heat, add enough coconut oil to cover the bottom of the pan by about ¼ in [6 mm], and let it preheat for a few minutes. Once the oil is hot but not smoking, add some of the breaded shrimp so they sit in an even layer with a little room between each.

Cook for 6 to 8 minutes total, flipping once halfway through (longer for large shrimp, shorter for small). The shrimp are done once they're golden brown on both sides and opaque all the way through. Remove to the lined plate and repeat with the remaining shrimp. Serve right away or store to reheat later (see storage).

Ways to use:
— With sweet chili sauce (page 112)
— Tucked into tacos with cabbage slaw (page 114)
— In katsu curry (page 116)
— Serve with gochujang sauce (page 181)
— Make a Thai red curry and top with coconut shrimp
— Top a bowl of grits with coconut shrimp and hot sauce

Coconut shrimp with sweet chili sauce

⏱ **5+ MIN**
◔ 15+ MIN
ⓘ 30+ MIN

About ¾ cup [190 g]

¼ cup [60 g] rice vinegar
¼ cup [60 g] water
3 Tbsp sugar
2 Tbsp sambal oelek
1½ tsp cornstarch
1 batch coconut shrimp (page 111)

Whip up a quick batch of sweet chili sauce, fry up some coconut shrimp, and enjoy as an appetizer. If you're pressed for time, you can always use store-bought sweet chili sauce, but I love making my own homemade version, so I can make it extra spicy.

———————

Place the vinegar, water, sugar, sambal oelek to taste, and cornstarch in a small saucepan. Whisk together off the heat until the cornstarch is completely lump-free.

Place over medium heat and bring to a simmer, whisking occasionally. As it begins to reach a simmer, start whisking constantly. Once it simmers for about 1 minute, remove from the heat—it should have thickened and become clear. Chill and then enjoy.

Make-ahead instructions
This sauce will keep in the fridge
for about 1 week.

Coconut shrimp tacos with cabbage slaw

⏱ 5+ MIN
🕐 **15+ MIN**
⏲ 30+ MIN

8 tacos

6 cups [390 g] thinly shaved
    cabbage
2 Tbsp chopped fresh cilantro
2 Tbsp mayonnaise
1 Tbsp lime juice, plus more for
    sprinkling
1 tsp lime zest
1 garlic clove, crushed through
    a press
Salt
1 large avocado
1 batch coconut shrimp (page 111)
8 corn tortillas

My last book, *A Dish for All Seasons*, has an entire section on Baja fish tacos, so it's safe to say I'm a fan of tacos + seafood. Coconut shrimp is so flavorful on its own, it doesn't need much more than a simple slaw and some avocado.

———

Place the cabbage, cilantro, mayonnaise, lime juice, lime zest, garlic, and about ¼ tsp salt in a medium mixing bowl. Toss together until coated very evenly. Set aside.

Slice the avocado into a separate mixing bowl. Sprinkle with a little lime juice, as needed. Toss together to evenly coat. Set aside.

Once the coconut shrimp have been fried, place one tortilla on a plate in the microwave, and microwave for just a few seconds until warm. You can also warm the tortillas in an ungreased skillet or over a gas flame. They should be flexible and delicious. Top each tortilla with a heap of slaw, a few shrimp, and some avocado. Enjoy right away.

Make-ahead instructions
Components (including the slaw) can be prepped the day before and then assembled at the last minute.

Other components you can use
To make these vegetarian, replace the shrimp with garlicky mushrooms (page 77) and add a little bit of Cotija cheese. Also try skipping the avocado and drizzling on a little avocado tomatillo salsa verde (page 163) instead.

Katsu curry with coconut shrimp

When you want to make Japanese curry rice, the best way to start is with store-bought curry roux cubes. I learned this from my friend Nami's blog (*Just One Cookbook*), tried it at home, and was totally convinced. Curry roux cubes are a little hard to track down, which might make this recipe a bit more of a project for anyone who doesn't live near an Asian market. But once you get home, you're halfway to a comforting dinner.

———

⏱ 5+ MIN
◔ 15+ MIN
ⓘ **30+ MIN**

6 servings

For the rice:
3 cups [600 g] medium-grain rice
3¾ cups [880 g] water plus more for rinsing
1½ tsp salt

For the curry:
1 Tbsp neutral oil (such as canola or avocado)
1 large or 2 small onions, thickly sliced
2 carrots, cut into ½ in [13 mm] chunks
1 russet potato, cut into ½ [13 mm] chunks
3½ cups [820 g] water
6 pieces [115 g] medium hot Vermont Curry (see recipe note), plus more as needed
1 batch coconut shrimp (page 111)

To make the rice, place the rice in a medium saucepan. Cover with some cold water, swish around well, and drain. Add the rice back to the saucepan and stir in the water and salt. Place over medium-high heat with the lid off (do not stir again). As soon as the rice comes to a simmer, place a lid on top and immediately lower the heat to low. (Now's a good time to start the curry.)

Simmer the rice, covered, for 15 minutes without peeking and without stirring. After 15 minutes, without uncovering the pan, remove from the heat and rest the rice or 10 to 20 more minutes. After it's rested, fluff the rice with a fork and serve immediately.

To make the curry, place a large sauté pan over medium heat. Once moderately hot, add the oil, swirl to coat, and add the sliced onion. Cook for about 10 minutes, stirring occasionally, until lightly golden and softened.

Add the carrots, potato, and water and increase the heat to high to bring to a simmer. Once simmering, lower the heat to medium-low and cook, uncovered, for about 10 minutes, until the veggies are more tender but still raw at the center.

Add the curry cubes and break them up with the back of a spoon. Let simmer for 5 more minutes, stirring frequently, until the potatoes and carrots are completely tender and easily pierced with a knife. The sauce should be thick and very flavorful (taste it—if it's too thin and bland, let it cook a little longer to reduce down or add another cube; add a little more water if it's too thick).

Place a scoop of rice off-center in a bowl, place a scoop of curry next to it, and then top with some of the shrimp. Repeat with the remaining ingredients and serve immediately.

Recipe note

You can find Vermont Curry at most Asian markets. If you can't find this exact brand, you can use another variety of Japanese curry sauce mix (but taste as you add it, as different brands will vary in flavor and strength; if you overdo it, just add a little more water).

Substitutions

Replace the coconut shrimp with the crispy chicken on page 160.

Turkey spinach meatballs

There are three keys to really good meatballs: First, salt them on the outside rather than the inside to make sure they turn out tender. Second, add a combination of bread crumbs and milk so they don't turn out dry. And third, deglaze the pan afterward to create a little pan sauce that clings to them. I love turkey, but you can substitute whatever ground meat you like here.

————

Makes 30 to 35 meatballs, enough to make any 1 recipe from this section

8 oz [225 g] frozen chopped spinach, thawed
1 lb [455 g] ground turkey
½ cup [55 g] bread crumbs
½ cup [30 g] finely grated Parmesan
⅓ cup [80 g] whole milk
1 Tbsp dried basil
3 garlic cloves, crushed through a press
1 tsp freshly ground black pepper
¾ tsp salt
1 Tbsp extra-virgin olive oil
¼ cup [60 g] water

Wring the spinach out well until it's very dry. You should end up with about 1 cup [110 g]. Add the spinach to a mixing bowl along with the turkey, bread crumbs, Parmesan, milk, basil, garlic, and pepper (do not add the salt). Mix together until well combined.

Shape into 30 to 35 heaped meatballs, about 1 Tbsp each. Set on a plate as you shape them, then sprinkle evenly on the first side with half the salt.

Heat a large nonstick sauté pan or well-seasoned cast-iron skillet over medium heat. Once hot, add the oil, swirl to coat, and add the meatballs salty-side down. Sprinkle the other side with the rest of the salt. Cook until deeply golden brown on one side before turning. Rotate the meatballs every couple minutes, for a total of about 10 minutes. Once evenly seared, add the water to the pan, cover, and steam the meatballs for about 3 more minutes, until completely cooked through. Remove the lid and let the liquid reduce down while frequently shaking the pan to roll the meatballs around. Stop once the sauce glazes the meatballs, 2 to 3 minutes after removing the lid.

Storage
Meatballs last for 3 to 4 days in the fridge, or at least 3 months in the freezer in a tightly sealed container.

Ways to use:
— For cheesy meatball bake with spinach (page 120)
— In Italian wedding soup (page 122)
— With mashed potatoes and gravy (page 124)
— Use in place of the smoky eggplant in the Chicago-style deep-dish pizza on page 58
— Make the antipasto pasta salad on page 158 a bit more substantial with a few turkey spinach meatballs
— Make some classic Italian-American spaghetti and meatballs with your favorite red sauce

Cheesy meatball bake with spinach

Once you've got a batch of turkey spinach meatballs, you're only a few minutes away from a cheesy meatball bake. Just pour a jar of tomato sauce over, sprinkle with cheese, and broil until bubbly.

———————

⏱ **5+ MIN**
⊖ 15+ MIN
ⓘ 30+ MIN

4 servings alone or 6 with pasta

1 batch turkey spinach meatballs (page 119)
One 15 oz [425 g] container tomato sauce
1½ cups [150 g] shredded low-moisture mozzarella
½ cup [45 g] coarsely grated Parmesan
Cooked pasta, to serve (optional)

Set the oven to broil.

If your meatballs are in a broiler-proof 10 in [25 cm] cast-iron skillet, proceed with the recipe. If not, transfer to a pan that can go from stove to broiler. If starting with leftover meatballs, place them in a cast-iron skillet.

Pour the tomato sauce over the meatballs. Place over medium-high heat, just until the sauce starts simmering rapidly (let it simmer for about 2 minutes if the meatballs are cold). Sprinkle with the mozzarella and Parmesan. Place the skillet under the broiler until the whole thing is bubbly (this varies from oven to oven, but check on it every couple minutes). Serve on its own or over pasta.

Italian wedding soup

While not traditional, turkey spinach meatballs are lovely in Italian wedding soup, which is all about the marriage of greens and meat. For a more traditional version of this Italian-American meal, make the meatballs with ground pork, veal, or beef instead.

———————

⏱ 5+ MIN
◔ **15+ MIN**
ⓘ 30+ MIN

6 servings

2 Tbsp extra-virgin olive oil
3 carrots, chopped
1 onion, chopped
¼ tsp salt
1 batch turkey spinach meatballs (page 119)
2 qt [1.9 L] chicken stock
1 tsp dried basil
½ tsp freshly ground black pepper
1 cup [90 g] small pasta (such as ditalini)
8 oz [225 g] frozen chopped spinach, thawed and wrung out
Finely grated Parmesan, for serving

Place a stockpot over medium heat. Once moderately hot, add the oil, swirl to coat, and immediately add the carrots and onion. Season with the salt. Cook, stirring occasionally, for about 10 minutes, until softened.

Add the meatballs, chicken stock, basil, and pepper. Increase the heat to high and bring to a simmer. Once simmering, add the pasta and set a timer for 2 minutes less than the time on the package (it will coast the rest of the way off the heat). Add the spinach once the timer goes off, remove from the heat, cover, and let stand for a few minutes before serving. Serve in bowls with Parmesan at the table.

Make-ahead instructions
This soup keeps in the fridge for 2 to 3 days, or the freezer for at least 3 months.

Meatballs with mashed potatoes and gravy

⏱ 5+ MIN
⊖ 15+ MIN
ⓘ **30+ MIN**

5 servings

For the potatoes:
4 or 5 medium russet potatoes,
    peeled and cut into 1 in [25 mm]
    cubes
8 to 12 medium peeled garlic
    cloves
2 Tbsp unsalted butter
1 cup [240 g] buttermilk
½ tsp freshly ground black pepper
Salt

For the gravy and meatballs:
**1 batch turkey spinach meatballs
    (page 119)**
2 Tbsp unsalted butter
2 Tbsp all-purpose flour
1½ cups [350 g] chicken or
    vegetable stock
2 tsp fresh thyme leaves,
    plus more for serving
1 garlic clove, crushed through
    a press
Salt

The secret to delicious mashed potatoes is real buttermilk. While you can get away with a yogurt/milk substitute in baking, nothing else will cut it here for tang and richness. Add as much as you need to, until your potatoes are fluffy and silky smooth.

————

To make the mashed potatoes, bring a large stockpot of water to a boil. Once boiling, add the potatoes and garlic and lower the heat to medium to maintain a low boil. Let simmer for about 15 minutes, until you can easily pierce the potatoes and garlic with a fork. Drain and leave the potatoes and garlic in the stockpot off the heat.

Add the butter and mash together until the butter has melted and the potatoes and garlic are completely mashed. Add the buttermilk, pepper, and salt to taste (about 1 tsp) and stir together. When ready to serve, reheat over low heat while stirring constantly, or in the microwave.

To make the gravy, if you just made the meatballs, remove all but one from the pan. If you're starting with leftover meatballs, place one meatball in a sauté pan. Place the butter in the pan with the meatball and set over medium heat. Once the butter melts, smash the meatball with the back of a wooden spoon. Stir frequently, breaking it up into smaller pieces with the spoon, until the pan has lots of broken-up brown bits, 2 to 4 minutes.

Add the flour, stir together for about 1 minute until the flour thins out, and immediately pour in the stock. Whisk together and let it cook until it simmers and thickens, about 2 minutes. Add the thyme and garlic and let it simmer for a few seconds just to meld the flavors. Season with salt to taste and remove from the heat.

Place some mashed potatoes in a bowl, swirl to create indentations, top with meatballs, and drizzle on some gravy. Top with more thyme and enjoy.

Make-ahead instructions
The mashed potatoes can be made ahead and reheated (add more buttermilk if they are too thick).

Other components you can use
Use whole roasted garlic (page 61) in place of the garlic cloves that simmer with the potatoes. Simply add the roasted garlic to the potatoes after straining them.

Lemongrass beef

There are more complicated lemongrass beef recipes out there, but I love this minimalist approach. Simply blend lemongrass, fish sauce, and a tiny bit of brown sugar, and marinate thinly sliced beef in the mixture. The most effective marinades cling to meat rather than wash over it; here, the lemongrass bits stick to the meat instead of only infusing it with flavor, so you can absolutely get away with a quick 30-minute rest.

_____

Makes 3 cups [370 g] seared beef, enough to make any 1 recipe from this section

1 lb [455 g] top sirloin
2 stalks lemongrass
3 Tbsp fish sauce
1 Tbsp brown sugar
Neutral oil, for cooking (such as canola or avocado)

Freeze the beef for 2 hours, so it's easier to slice thinly.

Remove the tough outermost leaves of the lemongrass. Cut off and discard the reedy stalk ends and the bit of root, saving only the tender light green part from the root side (you'll be left with about 1½ oz [40 g]).

Place the tender lemongrass in a food processor and blend until finely chopped. Add the fish sauce and brown sugar to the food processor and blend.

Once the beef is firm but not frozen solid, slice very thinly. Spoon the lemongrass mixture over the beef and toss together to evenly coat everything. Let sit for at least 30 minutes in the refrigerator (and for up to 2 days).

To sear on the stove, preheat a nonstick sauté pan over medium-high heat. Once hot, add about a teaspoon of oil, swirl to coat, and add about a sixth of the marinated beef. Spread it out into a single layer (do not crowd the pan). Let sear on one side until caramelized, then flip the pieces and sear the other side, 3 to 4 minutes total. Transfer to a container to cool and repeat with the remaining beef.

To grill, lightly oil the grill grates and preheat the grill to high. Thread slices of beef onto skewers in a ruched arrangement. Grill until charred and cooked through, 6 to 8 minutes total.

Storage
You can marinate the beef, refrigerated, for up to 2 days before cooking, or you can sear it and leave in the refrigerator for 4 to 5 days. To keep for at least 3 months, freeze in a tightly sealed container.

Ways to use:
— To fill lettuce cups (page 128)
— On skewers with peanut sauce (page 130)
— In bún (page 132)
— Add to the cold soba noodles on page 194
— Make a lemongrass beef banh mi
— Add to your favorite veggie stir-fry

Lemongrass beef lettuce cups

All you need is sautéed lemongrass beef and a big stack of floppy-crisp lettuce leaves to make a delicious little snack or appetizer. If you want to get extra fancy, you can also make the nuoc mam sauce on page 132 to dunk or drizzle.

———

⏱ **5+ MIN**
◔ 15+ MIN
ⓘ 30+ MIN

Separate your lettuce leaves, wash them, and spin them dry. Serve a heap of lettuce leaves with a bowl of lemongrass beef on the side. Use the leaves to scoop up pieces of beef.

6 servings as an appetizer

1 head butter lettuce or green leaf
  lettuce
**1 batch lemongrass beef, sautéed
  or grilled (page 127)**

Other components you can use
Coconut shrimp (page 111) makes a
great lettuce cup filling, especially
with a little sweet chili sauce
(page 112).

Lemongrass beef skewers with peanut sauce

6 servings as an appetizer

½ cup [130 g] creamy peanut
  butter
2 Tbsp soy sauce
2 Tbsp brown sugar
1 Tbsp plus 1 tsp rice wine vinegar
1 Tbsp chili garlic sauce or sriracha
1 tsp fish sauce
1 tsp sesame oil
2 Tbsp water
**1 batch lemongrass beef, skewered
  (page 127)**

Tips for entertaining, from an introvert: Skewer lemongrass beef and make a peanut sauce the day before, and then once the party starts, find the introverted person who made a beeline for your cat, and ask that guest if they'd mind grilling. It's a win/win: Your friend gets a 10-minute break, you can focus on whatever else you're making, and everyone gets some delicious satay while they wait.

———

In a small mixing bowl, stir together the peanut butter, soy sauce, brown sugar, vinegar, chili garlic sauce, fish sauce, and sesame oil. Add the water 1 Tbsp at a time, until it reaches your desired consistency. It will thicken slightly as it sits, but you can always thin it out a little later.

Grill your lemongrass beef once your sauce is ready, and serve on a plate with a little bowl for dipping.

Recipe note
If you're allergic to peanuts, try the
sesame ginger sauce on page 191.

Bún

There are a ton of amazing Vietnamese restaurants in Melbourne. My favorite is Lady Dan, where the bún is unbelievably good. If my take here is even half as good, it'll blow you away.

———

○ 5+ MIN
○ 15+ MIN
ⓘ **30+ MIN**

6 servings

For the nuoc mam:
¼ cup [60 g] lime juice
3 Tbsp fish sauce
3 Tbsp rice vinegar
2 Tbsp brown sugar
1 garlic clove, crushed through a press
1 or 2 Thai chiles, thinly sliced (optional)
¼ cup [60 g] water

For the bún:
6 oz [170 g] rice vermicelli
1 batch lemongrass beef (sautéed or grilled, page 127)
2 carrots, julienned
2 Persian cucumbers, thinly sliced
1 heart of romaine, thinly shredded
1 cup [45 g] packed fresh cilantro leaves
1 cup [25 g] packed fresh mint leaves
⅔ cup [40 g] chopped green onions
½ cup [20 g] fried shallots (see recipe note)
¾ cup [90 g] chopped peanuts or cashews
Lime wedges, for serving

To make the nuoc mam, in a small mixing bowl, combine the lime juice, fish sauce, vinegar, brown sugar, garlic, and chile, if using, and stir together until the sugar dissolves. Add half of the water, then add the rest gradually, tasting as you go and stopping once it tastes just right (light, tangy, funky, a little spicy, a little sweet).

To make the bún, cook the vermicelli according to the package instructions.

Divide the noodles among 6 bowls. Top each bowl with beef, carrots, cucumbers, romaine, cilantro, mint, green onions, fried shallots, nuts, and lime wedges. Serve with little bowls of nuoc mam on the side. Each guest should pour their sauce over their bún bowl and toss together right before eating.

Recipe note
You can find fried shallots at most Asian markets, but you can always make your own by pan-frying very thinly sliced shallots until golden brown. Cool on a paper towel–lined plate.

Make-ahead instructions
If you make this ahead, make sure you rinse your cooked noodles in cold water, strain, and coat in a tiny bit of oil so they don't stick together. All other components can be prepped ahead and stored for 2 days (vegetables together, onions and herbs together, everything else separately).

Dressings and sauces

Sauces and dressings are flavor itself. They're different from the vegetable, meat, and fruit components in this book because they're not substantial in the same way. Their lack of substance is both their strength and their weakness.

Think of sauces and dressings as pure electricity—you need to figure out a way to capture it and channel the energy. Once you do, you've got lightning in a bottle. You can throw a dressing or sauce on anything that begs for more flavor. To wield sauces well, you've got to be a little more thoughtful, so this section includes pairing notes to help with mixing and matching. Take these guidelines and make your way!

Consider these sensations when combining a dressing or sauce with a more substantial meat, fruit, vegetable, or starch:

1. Texture

Above all, consider the textures of the food you're pairing with a sauce, as sauces do not add much in the way of texture. Pay attention to crunch, creaminess, chewiness, and so on.

2. Flavor

Consider how your sauce's flavor might complement a dish. What flavors are missing, or what flavors do you want to enhance? For instance, the cilantro lime dressing (page 147) has a ton of herby flavor and a bit of acidity, so it wouldn't really do much to enhance something that's already extremely bright and herby, such as kuku sabzi (a zesty herb-packed Persian frittata). Instead, you might drizzle it over something that could use the acidity and herby flavor, like grilled red snapper. The sauces in this section vary a ton, so choose one with the right flavor profile for the food you plan to serve it with. Pay attention to how sweet, spicy, salty, tangy, savory, bitter, or even subtle the dish is, and then choose the right sauce to go with it.

3. Richness

Think about the richness of the sauce you're using: Rich sauces work well with light and crunchy ingredients, while a light and refreshing sauce will bring levity to heavier ingredients. Don't weigh down heavy ingredients with an even heavier sauce. And don't weigh down anything that might wilt with a super-heavy dressing.

Actually good vinaigrette

In 2019, food writer Samin Nosrat implored us all to add water to our vinaigrettes, and by gum, you bet I now often add water to my vinaigrette. Water solves an important problem: oil and vinegar are the two main ingredients in a vinaigrette, but oil and vinegar are both overwhelming in large quantities. So you can't balance out a vinaigrette by simply adding more or less of one or the other. That's where water comes in! Just a little bit helps smooth everything over.

But not all salads should get the water treatment. A vinaigrette made with water is just the thing for a greens-only salad such as the one on page 140. But if you're making a salad with lots of juicy ingredients (for instance, lots of tomato or cucumber), forgo the water. Moreover, if you're mixing up a big batch of vinaigrette at the beginning of the week, leave out the water, and splash some in as needed, depending on what ingredients you're coating.

———————

Makes ¾ cup [175 g], enough to make all 3 recipes in this section

½ cup [105 g] extra-virgin olive oil
1½ Tbsp balsamic or red wine vinegar
1½ Tbsp water (optional, see headnote)
1 Tbsp Dijon mustard
1½ tsp maple syrup
1 garlic clove, crushed through a press, or ½ tsp garlic powder
Salt

In a small mixing bowl, whisk together the olive oil, vinegar, water, if using, mustard, maple syrup, garlic, and salt to taste (¼ to ½ tsp). The mixture should stay emulsified for a little while, but you will need to shake it up or whisk it right before serving.

Storage
This dressing contains garlic and isn't extremely acidic, so it should only be stored in the fridge for a few days before consuming. But if you leave out the garlic and water, and add them later as needed, you can count on at least 1 week in the fridge.

Store-bought alternatives
Use your favorite store-bought vinaigrette.

Pairing notes
Use with foods that are already quite flavorful and just need acidity and richness. Acidity and richness highlight powerful flavors, so this vinaigrette is the missing puzzle piece for any salad that already has a lot to say.

Ways to use:
— For dressed greens with Pecorino or Parmesan (page 140)
— Drizzle on burrata with strawberries (page 144)
— With winter squash steaks (page 142)
— Dress a lobster salad
— Incognito olive salad on page 222
— Spinach salad on page 238
— Omit the water, increase the vinegar as needed, and brush onto bread to make an antipasto sandwich; if you're using greens, toss them lightly in some dressing too
— Include the water and use as a dipping sauce for whole artichokes (page 148)
— Omit the water and coat potatoes before roasting them
— Include the water and drizzle over grilled veggies; you can also include a few whole roasted garlic cloves (page 61)

Dressed greens with Pecorino or Parmesan

This is a green salad you'll actually want to eat. With a potable vinaigrette and a mountain of salty cheese, you don't even need tomatoes or croutons to liven things up. A tangle of perfectly seasoned greens is just the thing to accompany whatever else you're making. I like to use both finely grated cheese and big flakes—the fine gratings will coat the lettuce, and the big shavings add a contrast in texture.

⏱ **5+ MIN**
◔ 15+ MIN
◷ 30+ MIN

2 servings (easily doubles or triples)

2 giant handfuls (4¼ oz [120 g]) greens (for instance, arugula, frisée, or spring greens)
2 Tbsp actually good vinaigrette (page 139), made with water
Pecorino Romano or Parmesan
Coarse sea salt

Place the greens in a salad bowl and drizzle with vinaigrette. Use tongs to toss together until evenly coated.

Use a vegetable peeler and/or Microplane to shave and/or grate the cheese over the salad, to taste. Use the tongs to ruffle it a little (but don't fold or the cheese will fall to the bottom).

Sprinkle with sea salt and use a vegetable peeler to shave in a few big flakes of Pecorino Romano at the table.

Recipe notes
Always dress your salad at the very last minute. If you're using the vinaigrette and it already has water added, go right ahead and use it. If not, add about ¾ tsp water to 2 Tbsp undiluted vinaigrette for this recipe.

Make-ahead instructions
Mix up the vinaigrette up to a couple days ahead, wash and dry the lettuce and place it in the salad bowl the day before. Grate the cheese and place in a container. Store everything in the fridge, and bring it all together at the last moment.

Substitutions
You can use a sprinkle of nutritional yeast in place of the Pecorino Romano, which makes this salad vegan.

Other components you can use
The cilantro lime dressing (page 147) or creamy Caesar dressing (page 155) also work beautifully with a green salad. Don't add as much cheese if you use the creamy Caesar.

Winter squash steaks

You can use any firm-fleshed winter squash here. A medium butternut squash will work best for the following quantities, but if your squash is large, simply use extra feta, dates, rosemary, and (most importantly!) vinaigrette.

⏱ 5+ MIN
◔ **15+ MIN**
ⓘ 30+ MIN

8 servings

1 butternut squash
½ red onion, thinly sliced
3 Tbsp actually good vinaigrette (made without water, page 139), plus more for serving
¾ tsp salt
6 oz [170 g] ¼ in [6 mm] sliced feta
1 Tbsp chopped fresh rosemary needles, plus more for serving
8 pitted, halved Medjool dates (125 g)

Preheat the oven to 500°F [260°C].

Peel the butternut squash, slice off the stem, slice in half, and discard the seeds and pulp. Slice into about eight ¾ in [19 mm] thick wedges.

Line a rimmed sheet pan with parchment paper and place the squash and onion slices on it. Drizzle on the vinaigrette and use your hands to coat evenly. Arrange the squash in a single layer with space around each piece (use 2 sheet pans if necessary, and don't crowd the pan) and sprinkle with the salt. Layer the feta on and around the squash, and sprinkle with the rosemary.

Roast for about 20 minutes, until the feta is charred in spots and the squash has cooked through (stop before it gets mushy). Sprinkle on the dates after 15 minutes of roasting. Serve with a small sprinkling of rosemary needles (do not sprinkle whole sprigs), and drizzle with a little more vinaigrette, to taste.

Recipe note
While I'm calling for butternut squash here, this technique will work with just about any winter squash out there (but keep in mind that cook times will vary). Be careful not to overcook your squash, as they're not so delicious once they get mushy.

Other components you can use
Skip the rosemary, use olive oil to coat the squash instead of vinaigrette, and drizzle on the cilantro lime dressing (page 147) at the end instead.

Strawberry burrata

⏱ 5+ MIN
⊖ 15+ MIN
① **30+ MIN**

6 servings as an appetizer

For the almond brittle:
⅓ cup [65 g] sugar
¾ cup [105 g] almonds
¼ tsp ground cinnamon
¼ tsp cayenne pepper

For the burrata plate:
8 oz [225 g] burrata, strained
8 oz [225 g] strawberries, hulled
  and sliced
1 pint [300 g] cherry tomatoes,
  halved
**¼ cup [60 g] actually good
  vinaigrette (made without water,
  page 139)**
1½ Tbsp fresh thyme leaves

While it does take a little extra effort to make the savory almond brittle in this recipe, it's super easy to make a few days ahead of time. Throw everything else together at the last minute, and serve this crowd-pleaser small plate before the main course.

———

To make the almond brittle, line a sheet pan with parchment paper and place the ingredients within reach of the stove, because the steps of this recipe move quickly.

Place the sugar in a small saucepan and set over medium-high heat. Let it heat for about 2 minutes, until the edges and bottom start to melt and turn light amber. At this point, lower the heat to medium and begin stirring it constantly with a heatproof spatula.

Once the sugar becomes a runny amber liquid (about 2 minutes after the edges start to melt), lower the heat to low and continue cooking for 1 more minute while stirring constantly until it's completely lump-free, a little darker, and smells caramelly.

Add the almonds, cinnamon, and cayenne to the caramel, quickly stir together to coat evenly, and move to the prepared sheet pan as soon as the syrup is completely clinging to the almonds.

Flatten the almonds into a single layer with the spatula. Let cool for at least 20 minutes, then chop the brittle into pieces.

To assemble the burrata plate, place the burrata in the center of a serving plate. Surround it with the strawberries and tomatoes, drizzle on the vinaigrette, and sprinkle with the brittle and thyme leaves.

Make-ahead instructions
Make the brittle and vinaigrette up to 1 week ahead of time, then throw it all together at the last minute.

Cilantro lime dressing

This dressing is an absolute flavor bomb. While the actually good vinaigrette on page 139 is way more versatile, you're going to find reasons to put this one on everything. And I won't stop you! You can use any combination of basil, mint, parsley, or cilantro for a different flavor profile. And if you add an extra jalapeño and omit the water, you've got a delicious herby hot sauce.

———

Makes 2½ cups [590 g], enough to make all 3 recipes in this section

2 large bunches fresh cilantro, large stems removed

1 large or 2 small jalapeños, stemmed

6 garlic cloves

2 tsp lime zest

⅓ cup [80 g] lime juice

3 Tbsp water

2 Tbsp mayonnaise (optional, see recipe notes)

1 Tbsp maple syrup

1 tsp salt

1 tsp freshly ground black pepper

⅔ cup [140 g] extra-virgin olive oil

Place the cilantro, jalapeño, garlic, lime zest, lime juice, water, mayonnaise, if using, maple syrup, salt, and pepper in a high-powered blender (see recipe notes). Blend on medium speed until puréed.

With the blender running on medium speed, very slowly drizzle in the oil through the hole in the lid. The mixture will gradually lighten and thicken into a bright green salad dressing. Blend on high speed for a few more seconds, just to make sure it completely emulsifies.

Recipe notes
If you don't have a high-powered blender, you can make this in a food processor, regular blender, or immersion blender. You might not get it to emulsify with a food processor, but it will still taste amazing. Leaving out the mayo will also make it less likely to emulsify.

Storage
This dressing will last for about 1 day in the fridge, but it freezes for at least 3 months with no loss of quality. Freeze in small containers, then thaw by microwaving for about 30 seconds, just until it's the consistency of sorbet. Break it up with a fork, microwave for about 10 more seconds, stir, and let it coast the rest of the way.

Store-bought alternatives
While it will have a very different flavor profile from this recipe, you can turn store-bought pesto into a super-herby salad dressing by adding a tiny bit of balsamic vinegar until it tastes pleasantly tangy, thinning it out slightly with water, and adding a bit of salt and pepper.

Pairing notes
Use this cilantro lime dressing on any foods that need a big punch of flavor, a dose of acidity, and a tiny bit of richness. It goes great with anything that's a little plain on its own, and adds a zesty element to any salad that has lots of rich ingredients (for instance, egg, bacon, lettuce, and croutons).

Ways to use:
— With steamed artichokes (page 148)
— To dress escarole salad (page 150)
— Drizzled over Southwestern cobb salad (page 152)
— Serve over grilled steaks (see page 86) or pork chops (see page 254)
— Drizzle over a grain bowl with all your favorite vegetables (page 96)
— Use in place of salsa verde for huevos rancheros (page 166)
— Serve with crudités (see page 200)
— Make a salad with black beans, romaine, tomatoes, and lots of cilantro lime dressing
— Dress some greens and sprinkle with Cotija (see page 140 for a loose guide to dressing greens)
— Drizzle over grilled snapper

Steamed artichokes with cilantro lime dressing

Steamed artichokes with drawn butter will never go out of style, but artichokes also go surprisingly well with a variety of salad dressings. This bright green cilantro lime dressing is my favorite thing to include in a little condiment cup alongside a freshly steamed 'choke.

⏱ **5+ MIN**
◔ 15+ MIN
ⓘ 30+ MIN

6 servings as an appetizer

6 artichokes
1 cup [235 g] cilantro lime dressing (page 147)
Salt

Trim your artichoke stems down to the base, and ¾ in [19 mm] from the tip of each artichoke. Optionally, trim the very tip off each outer leaf (or just be careful when eating them later).

Place a steamer basket in a large stockpot and fill with 1 to 2 in [2.5 to 5 cm] of water so that the water almost reaches the base of the basket. Bring to a boil over high heat.

Once the water is boiling, add the artichokes with their leaves pointing downward, nesting them so there's room for the steam to move around them. Cover, lower the heat to low to maintain a low boil, and steam for 40 to 60 minutes. They're done once you can pierce through the stem to the heart with a skewer with little resistance.

Serve each artichoke with a little ramekin of cilantro lime dressing, seasoned to taste with a pinch of salt. Enjoy by dipping each leaf in the dressing and scraping off the meat with your front teeth, discarding the husks of the leaves. Once you get to the purple center and the leaves are no longer meaty, remove the center and the fuzz underneath. Scoop out the heart, dip it in the dressing, and enjoy.

Other components you can use
Toum (page 171) or vinaigrette (page 139) also makes a great dipping sauce.

Escarole salad

Eggs are best poached in the calmness of an empty kitchen, with nothing else going on, no hungry guests waiting, and plenty of space and time. Fortunately, they keep well in the fridge (see make-ahead note), so you can always make them in a moment of zen and then serve them in the chaos of entertaining. Best practices usually suggest using "the freshest eggs you can find," but if you (like me) don't live on a chicken farm, that's probably unrealistically precious. But don't sweat it—as long as you give them a quick strain to eliminate the watery bit of egg white, and as long as you carefully follow the recipe below, they'll turn out perfect every time.

———

⏱ 5+ MIN
◔ **15+ MIN**
ⓘ 30+ MIN

4 servings

For the poached eggs:
Bowl of cold water with a scoop of ice
2 qt [1.9 L] water
1 Tbsp white vinegar
1 tsp salt
4 large eggs

For the salad:
3 or 4 slices sourdough, cut into ¾ in [19 mm] cubes
2 tsp extra-virgin olive oil
Salt
7 pieces of bacon
1 small head curly endive or escarole, washed and chopped
1 cup [235 g] cilantro lime dressing (page 147)

To poach the eggs, set the bowl of ice water next to the stove. Fill a large saucepan with the water, vinegar, and salt and bring to a boil over high heat.

While you're waiting for it to come to a boil, strain your eggs: Place a small fine-mesh sieve over a bowl. Break an egg into the sieve, letting the watery outer whites strain away, leaving behind the thick whites and the yolk. Move the strained egg to a measuring cup with a pour spout. Repeat with the remaining eggs, and discard the runny whites.

Once the water comes to a boil, lower the heat to maintain a low boil. Hold the measuring cup in one hand and a slotted spoon in another. Vigorously stir the water in a circular motion, stop, wait 1 second, and pour one egg right into the center of the whirlpool, dropping it swiftly from just above the water's surface.

Immediately set a timer for 3 minutes. As soon as the timer goes off, remove the egg with a slotted spoon to the ice bath. Let it chill for at least 10 minutes, and remove from the ice water with a slotted spoon when you're ready to use it. Repeat with the remaining eggs.

To make the salad, preheat the oven to 350°F [180°C].

Place the bread on a sheet pan, drizzle it with the oil to coat evenly, spread it into an even layer, and sprinkle it with a pinch of salt. Place the bacon on a separate sheet pan. Place both sheet pans in the oven and bake for 20 to 25 minutes, until the croutons are golden brown and very crunchy, and the bacon is crisp and has rendered most of its fat.

Place the endive in a salad bowl and top with about ⅔ cup [160 g] of the dressing. Toss together to coat evenly. Top with the bacon, croutons, poached eggs, and about ⅓ cup [80 g] more dressing, as needed.

Make-ahead instructions
Poached eggs will keep in the
fridge for about 4 days submerged
in cold water in a sealed container.
Warm them by straining, pouring hot tap water over them, and
letting them sit for 3 to 4 minutes.
Croutons are best made the
day you plan to serve them.

Southwestern cobb salad

While I love a classic cobb salad, I usually feel like it's missing something, namely a super flavorful dressing. The salad itself is composed mainly of very mellow ingredients, so cilantro lime dressing is just the thing to kick it up a notch.

———————

⏱ 5+ MIN
⊖ 15+ MIN
ⓘ **30+ MIN**

4 servings

1 large or 2 small chicken breasts
Salt
Neutral oil, for cooking (such as avocado or canola)
4 large eggs (optional)
1 large avocado
2 tsp lime juice or apple cider vinegar
2 ears of corn, grilled or blanched (see recipe notes)
Outer leaves from 1 medium head romaine, chopped
½ cup [115 g] cilantro lime dressing (page 147)
½ pint [150 g] cherry tomatoes, halved
1 cup [60 g] broken tortilla chips or tortilla strips

At least 20 minutes before you plan to cook (and up to a few days ahead of time), prep your chicken to help it stay juicy: Butterfly the chicken breast by carefully cutting it in half horizontally, but leave one long side attached instead of cutting all the way through. Then open it like a book so it lies flat. Season the chicken on both sides with ¼ tsp salt and let it sit in the fridge.

Once your chicken is ready, set a nonstick sauté pan or skillet over medium-high heat. Once hot, add 1 tsp oil and swirl to coat. Add the chicken and let it cook for 8 to 9 minutes per side, until golden brown all over and cooked all the way through. Let the chicken cool on a plate, and then slice into bite-size pieces once it's cool enough to handle.

If using the eggs, set the pan back over medium heat, add another 1 tsp of oil, and crack the eggs into the pan. Season with a pinch of salt and cook for 2 to 3 minutes, until the whites are opaque but the yolks are still runny. Cover them while they cook if you want the tops of the whites to set more firmly. Transfer to a plate while you prep the rest of the salad.

Slice your avocado and toss the slices with the lime juice, then season with a pinch of salt. Slice the corn off the cobs.

In a large serving bowl, toss the romaine with about 6 Tbsp [85 g] of the dressing. Top with the chicken, avocado, corn, tomatoes, eggs, more dressing to taste, and the tortilla chips.

Recipe notes
To blanch whole cobs, just boil them for about 2 minutes, then shock them with cold water.
To grill whole cobs, follow the instructions on page 45. Or use an equal amount of thawed frozen corn kernels (1½ cups [210 g]).

Make-ahead instructions
You can sear the chicken a couple days ahead, or at least salt the chicken a couple days ahead to sear at the last minute. Prep all your components up to a couple days ahead, and then bring everything together at the last minute.

Substitutions
Use this salad as a jumping-off point and sub in whatever veggies and greens you have on hand. Try to substitute like for like (cucumbers for tomatoes, sweet potato for corn, etc.). This dressing works particularly well for heartier greens, so romaine or iceberg would work better than arugula.

Creamy Caesar dressing

This is not the kind of Caesar dressing made with anchovies and egg yolks, stirred up tableside by candlelight in an old-timey steak house. Instead it's a delicious homemade version of the kind from a bottle that you probably grew up with. It's got a ton of Parmesan and a decent amount of garlic, and it's delicious on hearty greens.

————

Makes 1¾ cups [420 g], enough to make all 3 recipes in this section

1½ cups [85 g] finely grated Parmesan
¾ cup [175 g] mayonnaise
¼ cup [60 g] red wine vinegar
2 Tbsp Worcestershire sauce
1½ Tbsp water
1½ Tbsp Dijon mustard
1½ Tbsp pressed or minced garlic
¾ tsp freshly ground black pepper
¼ to ½ tsp salt

Combine the Parmesan, mayo, vinegar, Worcestershire sauce, water, mustard, garlic, pepper, and salt in a jar or mixing bowl. Whisk or shake together until smooth and creamy.

Storage
This dressing lasts for about 5 days in the refrigerator in an airtight container.

Store-bought alternatives
You can use store-bought Caesar dressing for any of the recipes in this section (use it to taste, depending on how rich or creamy your store-bought version is).

Pairing notes
Use this creamy Caesar dressing with anything that could use a dose of richness, savoriness, acidity, and creaminess. It makes anything light and refreshing feel more substantial, and goes great with crunchy vegetables.

Ways to use:
— On crunchy cheesy kale (page 156)
— Folded into antipasto pasta salad (page 158)
— For Caesar with crispy chicken (page 160)
— Make the dressed greens on page 140 with this in place of the vinaigrette, but cut back on the Parmesan
— Make the incognito olive salad on page 222 with this in place of the vinaigrette
— Serve with crudités
— Make smash burgers with lettuce, tomato, pickles, American cheese, and a drizzle of this dressing instead of your usual burger sauce
— Dress a kale or cabbage slaw with this Caesar dressing
— Use in your favorite potato salad recipe in place of mayo or vinaigrette

Crunchy cheesy kale

My favorite way to cook kale as a side is somewhere between crisp and sautéed. This roasted kale is crispy in spots and chewy in others, and incredibly flavorful throughout. Or if you'd prefer, you can spread the leaves over two sheet pans in a single layer to make kale chips (just keep an eye on them and make sure they don't burn).

⏱ **5+ MIN**
◔ 15+ MIN
◔ 30+ MIN

4 servings

Leaves from 1 medium bunch
  Lacinato kale
**⅓ cup [80 g] creamy Caesar
  dressing (page 155)**
2 Tbsp finely grated Parmesan
  (optional)
Salt

Preheat the oven to 350°F [180°C].

Place the kale leaves on a parchment-lined sheet pan. Top with the dressing and massage the leaves with your hands until they're very evenly coated. Spread the leaves out into an even layer and sprinkle with Parmesan, if using. Season with salt, as needed.

Bake for 20 minutes, until crispy in some spots and chewy in others.

Make-ahead instructions
Wash, dry, and store the kale wrapped in a towel in a sealed container in the refrigerator for 1 to 2 weeks. Make the dressing up to 5 days ahead. Dress and roast the kale at the last minute.

Other components you can use
For a very different flavor, use ¼ cup [70 g] of the gochujang sauce on page 181 instead of the Caesar dressing. Gochujang kale can be made without the added cheese to make this dish vegan (gochujang sauce is almost always vegan, but do check the ingredients because it's occasionally made with fish).

Antipasto pasta salad

I'm pretty sure every single one of my Italian friends will slam the book shut and roll their eyes upon seeing this recipe, and I absolutely wouldn't blame them. "Antipasto pasta" makes absolutely no sense. And yet the combination of mozzarella, artichoke, salami, and basil in an American-style pasta salad is just plain delicious, especially with a tangy Caesar dressing. It has no business being this good.

⏱ 5+ MIN
◔ 15+ MIN
◓ 30+ MIN

6 large servings

Salt
12 oz [340 g] bowtie pasta
⅔ cup [160 g] creamy Caesar dressing (page 155)
One 12 oz [340 g] can marinated artichoke hearts, drained
1 pint [300 g] cherry tomatoes, halved
8 oz [225 g] mozzarella pearls, drained
¾ cup [105 g] pitted Castelvetrano olives
3 oz [85 g] thinly sliced spicy salami, cut into strips
1 red bell pepper, thinly sliced
1 shallot, very thinly sliced
1 small bunch fresh basil

Set a stockpot of lightly salted water over high heat. Once boiling, add the pasta and cook until al dente, according to the package instructions. Once the pasta is done, rinse under cold water, drain well, and move to a large mixing bowl. Top with about ⅓ cup [80 g] of the dressing, season to taste with salt, and stir together to coat evenly.

Add the artichoke hearts, cherry tomatoes, mozzarella pearls, olives, salami, bell pepper, and shallot. Tear most of the basil leaves while adding them to the bowl, reserving some for garnish. Top with the remaining ⅓ cup [80 g] of the dressing and more salt to taste and toss together. Transfer to a serving bowl, garnish with the remaining basil, and serve.

Make-ahead instructions
Leftovers keep great for a couple days in the fridge, but it's best put together at the last minute for guests. You can make the pasta, mix up the dressing, and prep the ingredients ahead of time, then bring everything together just before serving.

Other components you can use
You can add a few turkey spinach meatballs (page 119) to make this salad more substantial.

Caesar with crispy chicken

When you throw in some crispy chicken, you can absolutely serve Caesar salad as a main. The creamy Caesar dressing is light yet super flavorful, and it ties everything together.

———

⏱ 5+ MIN
⊖ 15+ MIN
ⓘ **30+ MIN**

4 servings as a main

3 or 4 slices crusty bread, cut into ¾ in [19 mm] cubes
Extra-virgin olive oil, for drizzling
Salt
1 lb [455 g] chicken breast
⅓ cup [45 g] all-purpose flour
1 large egg, beaten
1 cup [75 g] panko bread crumbs
Neutral oil, for frying (such as canola or peanut)
3 medium hearts of romaine, chopped
¾ cup [175 g] creamy Caesar dressing (page 155)

Preheat the oven to 350°F [180°C].

Place the bread on a sheet pan, drizzle with the oil to coat evenly, spread into an even layer, and sprinkle with a pinch of salt. Bake for 20 to 25 minutes, until the croutons are golden brown and very crunchy. Set the croutons aside, and save the sheet pan for later.

Slice each chicken breast into 3 long strips. Season evenly with a little more than ½ tsp salt (or to taste). Let it dry-brine for several minutes in the fridge while you set up a dredging station. Place the flour on a large plate, place the egg in a bowl, place the bread crumbs on a large plate, and place an empty plate at the end of the line.

Set a heavy sauté pan over medium heat on a back burner and fill with about ½ in [13 mm] of oil (leaving at least 1½ in [4 cm] of headroom to prevent boiling over). Line the reserved sheet pan with a wire rack and place it within arm's reach of the stove.

Pick up a piece of chicken, roll it in the flour, and shake it a little to remove any excess. Place it in the egg bowl, then roll it around to coat evenly. Move it to the bowl of bread crumbs and roll it around and pat to coat evenly. Place it on the empty plate and repeat with the remaining chicken strips.

Once your oil is hot enough (it will sizzle rapidly if you dip the end of a chicken strip in it), lower in about half the strips (do not crowd the pan). Fry for 3 to 4 minutes on each side, then transfer to the wire rack and sprinkle with salt. Check to make sure they are cooked all the way through (an internal temperature of 165°F [74°C]). If they are browning too quickly or not sizzling rapidly enough, adjust the heat.

Place the romaine in a salad bowl, top with about ½ cup [115 g] of the dressing, and toss together to coat evenly.

Place the crispy chicken on a cutting board, slice into bite-size pieces, top the salad with the chicken pieces and croutons, and drizzle with the remaining ¼ cup [60 g] of dressing.

Recipe note

When breading the chicken, reserve your left hand for dry ingredients and your right for wet ingredients to prevent buildup. This conserves ingredients and makes less of a mess.

Make-ahead instructions

To make ahead, you can store breaded chicken in the fridge in a sealed container for a couple days, and then fry it at the last minute. Wash, chop, and dry the lettuce and store it in a paper towel–lined container for a day or two. Make the dressing up to 5 days ahead, and bring everything together at the last minute.

Substitutions

Use store-bought frozen chicken fingers and ready-washed and chopped romaine for an easy shortcut.

Avocado tomatillo salsa verde

I love salsa verde in any form, but I'm always extra excited when I get to a taqueria and see a squeeze-bottle of extra-creamy avocado tomatillo salsa verde. If you're in a hurry, you can even make your own by doctoring a jar of salsa verde. Just look for one that lists tomatillos as one of the first ingredients, not green tomatoes. Throw the salsa in a blender with the flesh of 1 avocado, a little lime juice, cilantro, and salt (as needed), and enjoy.

Makes about 3 cups [680 g], enough to make all 3 recipes in this section

1 lb [455 g] tomatillos (about 10), hulled and rinsed
1 small or ½ medium white onion, peeled and quartered
1 serrano chile or 1 jalapeño, halved and stemmed
Neutral oil, for coating (such as canola or avocado)
1 ripe avocado, pitted and peeled
¼ cup [60 g] lime juice
¾ cup [30 g] packed fresh cilantro leaves
1 garlic clove
½ tsp salt

Preheat the broiler for a few minutes, just until the oven is hot.

Place the tomatillos, onion, and chile on a sheet pan and coat in a light layer of oil. Place under the broiler and cook until they soften and char, about 5 minutes.

Place the cooked produce in a food processor or blender along with the avocado. Add the lime juice, cilantro, garlic, and salt and blend until completely smooth and creamy.

Storage
Salsa verde will last for about 3 days in the fridge, or for at least 3 months in the freezer in a tightly sealed container with no loss of quality. Thaw in the fridge overnight, or microwave to thaw partially, then break up the semi-frozen mass with a fork and let sit in the fridge for 1 to 2 hours to fully thaw.

Store-bought alternatives
Use a store-bought avocado salsa verde or see headnote for instructions to doctor a jar of standard salsa verde.

Pairing notes
Use this salsa verde with foods that need a little herby tang, and are already quite rich on their own. It's amazing with eggs, tortilla chips, and red meat.

Ways to use:
— As a dip for chips and salsa verde (page 164)
— Atop huevos rancheros (page 166)
— In a steak salad (page 168)
— Use as a topping for pork chops (see page 254) or lamb chops (see page 228)

— Drizzle over a grain bowl
— Drizzle over the coconut shrimp tacos with cabbage slaw on page 114 (but skip the sliced avocado in that recipe)
— This salsa verde works phenomenally as a salad dressing, since it contains acidity, heat, and (crucially) fat
— Find a great recipe for chilaquiles verdes, and use this salsa for the salsa verde

Chips and salsa verde

This recipe could easily read: "Buy bag of tortilla chips, open bag of tortilla chips, serve with salsa." But in case you're looking for something 5 to 10 minutes more complicated, I've included instructions for frying your own tortilla chips. Whether you fry them yourself or crack open a bag, the avocado tomatillo salsa verde speaks for itself.

⏱ **5+ MIN**
◷ 15+ MIN
◷ 30+ MIN

Corn tortillas
Neutral high-smoke-point oil
  (such as canola, corn, or peanut)
Salt
**Avocado tomatillo salsa verde
  (page 163)**

Cut the corn tortillas into quarters or sixths (depending on how big they are). Line a plate or sheet pan with paper towels.

Place a couple of inches of oil in a large, heavy Dutch oven or stockpot and set over medium-high heat. Make sure it has plenty of room so it doesn't boil over, place it on a back burner in a spot where it can't be knocked over, and be very careful. Place a single piece of tortilla in the oil as it heats. Once the tortilla starts to brown, the oil is ready (discard that first one).

Carefully add a handful of tortilla wedges to the hot oil and immediately stir them with a slotted spoon to make sure they don't stick to each other. If the oil is moderately hot, they'll take about 3 minutes, and if the oil is very hot, they'll take about 1 minute and will be super blistered and puffed up. Control the heat as needed. Flip them once halfway through cooking, and fry just until they're golden brown and crisp. Remove with a slotted spoon to the paper towel–lined plate and immediately sprinkle with salt to taste. Repeat with the remaining tortillas, and serve with salsa.

Make-ahead instructions
Homemade chips are best the day of, but will last for a few days tightly sealed at room temperature.

Huevos rancheros

⏱ 5+ MIN
◔ **15+ MIN**
ⓘ 30+ MIN

2 tacos

2 tortillas
1 Tbsp butter
2 large eggs
Salt
Freshly ground black pepper
2 Tbsp avocado tomatillo salsa verde, for serving (page 163)
Fresh cilantro, for serving (optional)

Super minimalist huevos rancheros make an easy and delicious weekday breakfast. If you make the avocado tomatillo salsa verde and prep the ingredients ahead of time, all you've got to do is fry the eggs and assemble.

———

Place 1 tortilla directly over the burner on a gas stove set to high heat for about 10 seconds, then flip and cook for another 10 seconds (do not walk away, and do not let it catch on fire). If you don't have a gas stove, heat a sauté pan over medium-high heat. Cook each tortilla for about 30 seconds per side. Be careful not to let them dry out, and stop as soon as they are warm and flexible. Set aside and repeat with the other tortilla.

Place a nonstick sauté pan over medium-high heat and let it preheat. Once hot, add the butter. Swirl to melt and coat. Immediately crack the eggs into the pan, leaving enough space between each to avoid sticking together. Sprinkle with salt and pepper to taste, cover with a lid, and cook for about 2 minutes.

Check for doneness by gently poking the yolk with your finger (it should be wobbly) and poking a white with the spatula (it should not run). Transfer each egg to a tortilla.

Top each egg with salsa and a few leaves of cilantro, if using, and enjoy.

Other components you can use
These are also lovely with the cilantro lime dressing (page 147), but it's a lot richer, so use only about ½ Tbsp per tortilla.

Steak salad with salsa verde

Most salsas will very happily dress a salad, and since the best dressings usually have both fat and acidity, avocado tomatillo salsa verde is a particularly good contender.

⏲ 5+ MIN
◔ 15+ MIN
ⓘ **30+ MIN**

4 servings as a main

For the steak:
14½ oz [410 g] skirt or strip steak
Salt
¼ cup [55 g] avocado tomatillo salsa verde (page 163)

For the salad:
9 oz [255 g] kale leaves from about 2 medium bunches
1 cup [225 g] avocado tomatillo salsa verde (page 163)
1 pint [300 g] cherry tomatoes, halved
1½ cups [210 g] grilled corn kernels, from about 2 ears (page 45)
½ red onion, thinly sliced
1¼ cups [150 g] crumbled queso fresco
1 handful [60 g] tortilla chips, crushed

To make the steak, season the steak with ½ tsp salt. Coat in the avocado tomatillo salsa verde and let chill for at least 15 minutes and up to 2 days.

When you're ready to make the salad, grill the steak. Lightly oil the grill grates and preheat it to high. Once it's heated, place the steak on the grill and cook for about 3 minutes per side, until medium-rare. Transfer to a plate to rest and cool.

Once the steak has rested, slice into strips against the grain. Set aside.

To make the salad, place the kale in a salad bowl and top with about ½ cup [115 g] of the salsa. Wash your hands well and massage the kale. Top with the tomatoes, corn, red onion, queso fresco, chips, and steak, and drizzle with the rest of the salsa. Finish with a little more salt, as needed.

Recipe note
You can sear the steak on the stove instead of grilling it. Open a window, turn on your exhaust, and preheat a cast-iron skillet over high heat to make sure you get a good sear.

Make-ahead instructions
You can sear the steak and let it rest in the fridge for a few hours if you'd like (it's great cold in a salad). Prep the components ahead of time, then assemble at the last minute.

Toum

Toum is a garlic emulsion made throughout the Middle East and North Africa. It's got a sharp raw-garlic flavor, and it takes on a completely different flavor when you cook with it. Since its three main ingredients are garlic, oil, and lemon juice, it's a trifecta of umami/fat/acid. It works best when you want to coat something in a nice amount of fat and lots of garlicky flavor.

Makes 2 cups [460 g], enough to make all 3 recipes in this section

⅔ cup [100 g] peeled garlic cloves (see recipe notes)
¼ tsp salt
2 Tbsp cold water
1¼ cups [270 g] neutral oil (see recipe notes)
¼ cup [60 g] cold lemon juice

Combine the garlic and salt in a high-powered blender (see recipe notes for using a food processor). Blend at low speed until the garlic is coarsely puréed. Add the water and blend at medium speed until it breaks down further.

Remove the cap from the lid (but keep the lid on for safety), and with the blender running at medium speed, drizzle in about half of the oil very slowly through the small opening. Try to aim the stream of the oil for the center of the blades. Do not pour the oil too quickly or the emulsion will break—it should take a couple minutes.

Once you've added half of the oil, slowly drizzle in half of the lemon juice with the machine running.

Resume slowly drizzling in some of the oil until it thickens up dramatically (you may need to adjust the speed if it develops an air bubble from being too thick). Then slowly drizzle in the other half of the lemon juice with the machine running, and finish with the rest of the oil.

Recipe notes
Be sure to use the freshest garlic you can find. Old garlic cloves will look slightly wrinkly and will have green sprouts on the inside. Old garlic is better used for whole roasted garlic (page 61).

Do not double this recipe. Toum is an eggless emulsion, so it's very temperamental, and will break very easily. It must be made in small batches.

Turn the blender off while you're not adding ingredients to keep it from overheating.

Do not use extra-virgin olive oil for this (though you can use a super refined light olive oil). I like to use canola, but any other neutral oil will work. Refined avocado oil will give it a very slight avocado oil taste, but works well enough if you're looking for the healthiest possible option.

If you don't have a high-powered blender, you can easily make toum in a food processor instead. Make sure you mince the garlic finely with the salt, and then slowly add the water until it's completely puréed, and proceed.

cont'd

Storage

This toum will keep in the refrigerator for about 1 week. Do not freeze or it will separate.

Store-bought alternatives

Some fancier grocery stores sell refrigerated toum. Aioli would work as well, though it is not exactly the same. But if you're looking to make any of the three recipes in this book's toum section and really can't be bothered, plain old store-bought mayo mixed with a few cloves of crushed garlic will work great. It might sound a bit retro, but it works wonderfully for roasting chicken, roasting potatoes, and (of course!) slathering on BLTs. It's undeniably not toum, but it's certainly tasty.

Pairing notes

Use toum with any food that needs a hit of richness and flavor and just a little acidity. It's particularly good with chicken, fish, and other lean meats.

Ways to use:

— Coat crispy toum potatoes (page 174)
— Spread on a garlicky PLT (page 176)
— Use as a chicken marinade (see page 178)
— Slather elotes preparados with toum instead of mayo (page 46)
— Use on the pizza bianca ai funghi on page 82 instead of the whipped cream mixture
— Try using a smaller amount of toum in place of the dressing for a vegan version of the crunchy cheesy kale on page 156, and omit the additional Parmesan
— Steam artichokes (see page 148) and serve with toum for dipping
— Spread the outside of a grilled cheese with toum before frying
— Make moules-frites: Elevate a bag of frozen fries with a toum dipping sauce and white wine–steamed mussels
— If you're a fan of mayo on cheeseburgers, try some toum instead
— If you keep a vegan diet, try a garlicky Southern tomato sandwich instead of a BLT: Start with two slices of white bread, slather with toum, add slices of ripe summer tomatoes, top with salt and pepper, and enjoy

Crispy toum potatoes

This recipe has a toum double-whammy: Coat the potatoes in toum before roasting, and then serve them with toum as a dipping sauce. The garlicky flavor develops beautifully in the oven, and the flavor of the dipping sauce reintroduces that sharp raw-garlic flavor after roasting.

———————

5+ MIN
15+ MIN
30+ MIN

Peeled russet potatoes
Toum (page 171)
Salt
Freshly ground black pepper

Preheat the oven to 425°F [220°C].

Cut the potatoes into ½ in [13 mm] wedges and coat them in a generous layer of toum. Place the potatoes on a sheet pan in a single layer (do not crowd the pan, and use multiple sheet pans if you're making a lot). Sprinkle with salt and pepper to taste, and roast for about 40 minutes, until golden brown on the outside and fluffy on the inside. Serve with extra toum at the table.

Substitutions
For a quick shortcut, try using mayo with crushed garlic instead. Also try this with carrots and parsnips.

Garlicky PLTs

If you like your BLT with a little mayo, allow me to introduce you to your new favorite sandwich. It's got crispy pancetta, shredded lettuce, ripe tomatoes, and garlicky toum on each slice of bread. Or leave out the pancetta for a garlicky vegan version of a Southern tomato sandwich.

⊘ 5+ MIN
⊝ **15+ MIN**
ⓘ 30+ MIN

4 sandwiches

20 thin pancetta slices
2 tomatoes, thinly sliced
Salt
8 slices white sandwich bread
¼ cup [55 g] toum (page 171)
1 head baby romaine, finely
  shredded

Place a few pancetta slices in a single layer in a wide sauté pan. Set over medium heat and cook until browned on the first side (about 5 minutes after it starts to sizzle). Flip and cook for about 2 minutes on the second side, just until crisp-chewy. Repeat with the remaining pancetta, working in batches. It will take more like 2 to 3 minutes per side once oil collects.

While the pancetta is crisping up, place the tomato slices on a clean tea towel or a couple paper towels and season with a big pinch of salt. After about 5 minutes, dab them gently to sop up a bit of their moisture.

Lightly toast the bread, then assemble the sandwiches: Spread about ½ Tbsp of the toum on each slice of bread. Top one slice with pancetta, then tomato, then lettuce, and top with the other piece of bread. Add a couple toothpicks if you'd like, slice diagonally, and enjoy.

Make-ahead instructions
Fry the pancetta, prep the tomatoes and lettuce, and store in separate containers in the refrigerator for a few days.

Other components you can use
The creamy Caesar dressing (page 155) can replace the toum for a creamier sandwich. Use a smaller amount of caramelized tomatoes (page 101) in place of the fresh tomatoes for more umami.

Toum thyme chicken

⏱ 5+ MIN
◔ 15+ MIN
① **30+ MIN**

4 servings

⅓ cup [75 g] toum (page 171),
   plus more for serving
Salt
2 Tbsp fresh thyme leaves,
   plus more for serving
3 to 4 lb [1.4 to 1.8 kg] whole
   chicken

Salty toum is my new favorite way to dry-brine a chicken. The chicken becomes completely infused with garlic flavor the longer it sits in the fridge, and you don't have to coat it in oil or baste it once you go to roast it. Serve it with more toum at the table, and enjoy the garlicky goodness.

———————

Season the toum with a very generous amount of salt: Use 1¾ to 2¼ tsp of salt (a little over ½ tsp of salt per 1 lb of bone-in meat, or 1 g of salt per 130 g of bone-in meat). Stir the thyme into the salty toum.

Smear the chicken under the skin, on top of the skin, and inside the cavity with the seasoned toum. Cover and place in the refrigerator for at least 3 hours and up to a couple days.

Once the chicken is ready to roast, preheat the oven to 425°F [220°C].

Transfer the chicken to a small rimmed sheet pan or large ovenproof skillet. Place the chicken in the oven and bake for 60 to 90 minutes total, until the chicken registers an internal temperature of 165°F [74°C]. Let the chicken rest for about 10 minutes before carving, and serve with more toum and thyme at the table.

Make-ahead instructions
You can coat your chicken with the toum-salt mixture and leave it for a couple days in the refrigerator to dry-brine. All of the salt you use in the coating will end up in the chicken, so as long as you begin with the right amount of salt, you don't have to worry about the chicken getting saltier as it sits. I like to dry-brine my chicken right when I get it home from the super-market, and then roast it whenever I get around to it.

Substitutions
If you don't have toum on hand, you can still make this recipe with mayo mixed with crushed garlic. Use a pinch less salt, since mayo tends to be well seasoned. If you don't have fresh thyme leaves, use 2 tsp dried instead.

Gochujang sauce

Gochujang is a Korean fermented red pepper paste. It's a little sweet with a lot of smoky spice. If you're even a little familiar with Korean food, you've probably experienced gochujang in the sauce you drizzle over bibimbap (usually made with gochujang paste, vinegar, sugar, and sesame oil—pretty much exactly what you'll find in this recipe). The spicy, tangy, sweet combination means that you can use gochujang sauce anywhere you might use barbecue sauce or something similar.

_____

Makes 2⅔ cups [680 g], enough to make all 3 recipes in this section

1 cup [320 g] gochujang paste
¾ cup [175 g] rice wine vinegar
½ cup [100 g] sugar (see recipe note)
2 Tbsp soy sauce
2 Tbsp sesame oil
4 garlic cloves, crushed through a press

In a medium mixing bowl, whisk together the gochujang paste, vinegar, sugar, soy sauce, sesame oil, and garlic.

Recipe note
You can cut the sugar in half if necessary, though keep in mind that the one serving of gochujang sauce drizzled over bibimbap only has about 2 tsp [8 g] of granulated sugar. I've also made a very low-sugar version of this with a small amount of Splenda instead of granulated sugar. Just make sure to start out with a very small amount, as Splenda tends to be more potent than sugar. Add it just a little at a time, stopping once the flavor is heightened but it doesn't taste overtly sweet.

Storage
Gochujang sauce keeps for about 1 week in the refrigerator, or for at least 3 months in the freezer in a tightly sealed container with no loss of quality. Gochujang paste, on the other hand, lasts for over a year in the refrigerator, so keep it on hand.

Store-bought alternatives
Remember that gochujang (paste) is just an ingredient in gochujang sauce, so don't use them interchangeably. But you can sometimes find gochujang sauce sold in bottles (sometimes marketed as bibimbap sauce). Look for one that has some body and isn't too runny, and use it as needed in the recipes in this section (but note that its flavor might be different).

Pairing notes
Use this gochujang sauce with anything that could use a little spice, savoriness, sweetness, and acidity. It goes exceptionally well with rich ingredients (beef, pork, and egg).

Ways to use:
— For gochujang clams (page 182)
— In gochujang meatloaf (page 184)
— Atop bibimbap (page 186)
— Serve on the side with coconut shrimp (page 111)
— Coat the crunchy cheesy kale on page 156 with ¼ cup [70 g] of gochujang sauce instead of Caesar dressing
— Drizzle over grilled corn (page 45), grilled steak (page 86), or a mushroom omelette (page 78)
— Glaze meatballs with gochujang sauce
— Fry firm tofu in a little oil in a nonstick skillet until lightly browned and warmed through, pour on enough gochujang to coat, flip once or twice to coat evenly, cook until caramelized, and serve with more gochujang sauce on top, as needed
— Find a recipe for foil-wrapped baby back ribs that uses barbecue sauce, and use gochujang sauce in its place (skip the rub if it includes one in addition to barbecue sauce, and be sure to season your ribs with salt as needed)

Gochujang clams

My favorite city to visit is Busan, South Korea, and my favorite thing to eat there is seafood, whether at the Jagalchi Market stalls or the seaside spots selling cheesy grilled shellfish. These gochujang clams are inspired by all those trips to Korea where I ate my body weight in both clams and gochujang, usually separately, but here together.

⏱ **5+ MIN**
◔ 15+ MIN
ⓘ 30+ MIN

2 servings as an appetizer

1 lb [455 g] live clams, purged of sand
½ cup [130 g] gochujang sauce (page 181)

Rinse your clams very well and discard any ones with cracked shells or ones that are flopped open.

Place the gochujang sauce in a small stockpot or Dutch oven and bring to a simmer over medium heat. As soon as it starts simmering (do not wait or it will scorch), add your clams, cover with a tight-fitting lid, and cook for 5 to 6 minutes. The clams are done once they've all popped open (discard any ones that don't pop open). Toss them around in the gochujang sauce and serve immediately, pouring any remaining sauce over them.

Recipe note
Most live clams are sold already purged (ask if you're unsure). If they haven't been purged, just place them in a strainer basket in a bowl, cover with cool salt water, let them sit for about 30 minutes, lift the strainer out of the bowl, and discard the sandy water.

Substitutions
You can use this same technique for mussels.

Gochujang meatloaf

⊘ 5+ MIN
⊖ **15+ MIN**
ⓘ 30+ MIN

About 6 servings

2 tsp neutral oil (such as canola or
  avocado), plus more for greasing
  the pan
1 onion, chopped
1 cup [75 g] panko bread crumbs
**⅓ cup [95 g] gochujang sauce
  (page 181), plus more for glazing
  and serving**
¼ cup [60 g] milk
1 large egg
1½ tsp salt
1 lb [455 g] ground beef (90% lean)
1 lb [455 g] ground pork (90% lean)

Meatloaf loves a ketchupy glaze, but I don't particularly love ketchup, so I don't usually love meatloaf. But since this book's gochujang sauce checks a lot of the same flavor-profile boxes as ketchup, it works particularly well in and on meatloaf. It's sweet and tangy, with a good dose of spice and smoke.

———

Preheat the oven to 350°F [180°C]. Oil a 4 by 8 in [10 by 20 cm] loaf pan.

Place a medium sauté pan over medium heat, add some oil, swirl to coat, and add the onion. Cook, stirring occasionally, for about 10 minutes, until soft and lightly brown. Transfer to a mixing bowl.

Add the bread crumbs, gochujang sauce, milk, egg, and salt to the mixing bowl and stir to combine. Let sit until the liquid is completely absorbed by the bread crumbs. Add the ground beef and pork and use your hands to combine until completely incorporated (but do not overmix).

Transfer to the loaf pan and press into a compact, flat layer. Trace around the pan with just the edge of your thumb to create a little moat (sort of like making a souffle). Brush the whole thing with about 2 Tbsp more gochujang sauce (don't double-dip).

Bake for about 70 minutes, until the center is cooked through completely (the internal temperature should be 160°F [71°C]). Remove from the pan (discard any rendered fat and juices), drizzle with a little more gochujang sauce, slice, and serve with more sauce at the table.

Recipe notes
You can use a 5 by 10 in [13 by 25 cm] pan, noting that it will cook through a few minutes earlier. I've also made this meat loaf with ground turkey breast, which is also delicious.

Make-ahead instructions
You can form the loaf, leave it in the fridge covered, and bake it up to a day later.

Substitutions
You can also use whatever kinds of ground meat you'd like for this recipe, but note that a higher fat mix (for instance 80% lean) will lead to quite a lot of fat rendering from the loaf.

Bibimbap

I'm not going to lie and say that bibimbap is easier than you might think, because this is definitely one of the most time-consuming recipes in this book. But this recipe does have its benefits: First, you can make it ahead with no loss of quality. Just prep the components, store them, and then fry the rice and eggs right before assembling. Second, you can breeze through the whole recipe using just one sauté pan. And finally (and most importantly) it is absolutely delicious and worth every minute.

———————

To make the beef, place the sirloin in the freezer for 2 hours to make it easier to slice.

Once the beef is firm but still sliceable, slice very thinly and place in a bowl. Top with the apple, garlic, soy sauce, sesame oil, and brown sugar, toss together to coat evenly, and let sit for at least 30 minutes, and up to overnight.

Place a large nonstick sauté pan over medium-high heat for a few minutes. Once hot, add the beef, marinade and all. Stir frequently for 10 to 15 minutes, until the liquid evaporates and the meat caramelizes. Transfer the beef to a container and give the pan a quick rinse.

To make the vegetables, place the pan back over medium-high heat. Once hot, add about 1 tsp of the sesame oil, followed immediately by the zucchini, the brown sugar, and about 2 tsp of the soy sauce. Toss together for about 1½ minutes, until the sugar has melted and the zucchini has softened and browned a little. Tranfser to a container and set the pan back over medium-high heat.

Immediately add another 1 tsp of the sesame oil, followed by the carrots and the remaining 2 tsp of the soy sauce. Toss together for about 3 minutes, until the carrots have softened and browned. Transfer to the veggie container and set the pan back over medium-high heat.

Immediately add the remaining 1 tsp of sesame oil, followed by the mushrooms and ¼ tsp of salt. Let them cook down for 10 to 12 minutes, until the mushrooms give off their liquid, the liquid evaporates, and they brown nicely. Transfer to the veggie container. **cont'd**

⏱ 5+ MIN
⊖ 15+ MIN
① **30+ MIN**

6 servings

For the beef:
1 lb [455 g] top sirloin
1 green apple, grated
3 garlic cloves, crushed through
   a press
3 Tbsp soy sauce
2 Tbsp sesame oil
1 Tbsp brown sugar

For the vegetables:
3 tsp sesame oil
1 zucchini, julienned
1 tsp brown sugar
4 tsp soy sauce
3 carrots, julienned
1 lb [455 g] cremini mushrooms,
   thinly sliced
Salt

For the scorched rice:
1 tsp neutral oil (such as canola
   or avocado)
3 cups [600 g] medium-grain rice,
   cooked as on page 116 (chilled
   or made fresh)

To assemble:
2 Tbsp neutral oil
6 large eggs
Salt
**1⅓ cups [340 g] gochujang sauce
   (page 181)**
Sesame seeds, for garnish

To make the scorched rice, rinse out your nonstick skillet to get rid of any brown bits, and place it back over medium-high heat.

Once hot, add the oil, swirl to coat, and place half of the cooked rice in an even layer (do not stir it into the oil). Cover and let it cook for about 8 minutes without ever stirring. Lift the edge of the rice to check on it after about 5 minutes—once you see a golden brown crust with a couple darker brown spots, it's done. Transfer the rice to a container, repeat with the next batch, and then set the pan over medium heat for the eggs.

To assemble, first cook the eggs (only cook as many as you plan to serve right away). Place the oil in the pan, swirl to coat, crack your egg(s) into the pan, and season with a pinch of salt. Cook for 2 to 3 minutes, until the whites are set and the yolks are still runny.

Divide the scorched rice among 6 bowls, followed by the vegetables and beef. Top each bowl with about 2 Tbsp of the gochujang sauce, an egg, and a sprinkling of sesame seeds.

Make-ahead instructions

Prep the components and store them in 4 separate containers: sautéed beef, sautéed vegetables, rice, and gochujang sauce. Scorch the rice and fry the eggs once you're ready to serve, heat the beef and vegetables in the microwave, and assemble at the last moment.

Substitutions

You can incorporate some corn and/or sautéed spinach in place of some of the veggies. Also feel free to choose a different meat—pork and chicken work well here too, though cook times will vary. To make this vegetarian, use miso sweet potatoes (page 93) in place of the beef.

Sesame ginger sauce

If you're not accustomed to working with it, tahini can be a little unpredictable. It starts out very runny, then thickens dramatically with a few drops of water, and then it thins back out with enough additional liquid. This recipe takes advantage of that, with just enough liquid to make a sauce that coats vegetables perfectly with lots of sesame ginger flavor.

_____

Makes 2¾ cups [660 g], enough to make all 3 recipes in this section

1 cup [250 g] tahini
¾ cup [175 g] water
⅓ cup [80 g] rice vinegar
3 Tbsp soy sauce
2 Tbsp honey
2 Tbsp sesame oil
1 Tbsp lime juice
3 Tbsp minced fresh ginger
3 garlic cloves, crushed through
  a press

In a medium mixing bowl, whisk together the tahini, water, vinegar, soy sauce, honey, sesame oil, lime juice, ginger, and garlic. It will start out watery, but will thicken as you continue to whisk, and will thicken further in the refrigerator.

Storage
This sauce will keep for 3 to 4 days in the fridge, or at least 3 months in the freezer in a tightly sealed container.

Pairing notes
Use this sesame ginger sauce with anything that would benefit from an aromatic, umami flavor and a little acidity. It's especially good with bland and starchy foods or light and refreshing vegetables, especially when served with little lime wedges for some additional acidity. Sesame ginger sauce also loves herby flavor, especially cilantro, basil, and mint.

Ways to use:
— With baked sweet potatoes (page 192)
— For cold soba noodles (page 194)
— For dipping spring rolls (page 196)
— Try in place of the peanut sauce on page 130 with lemongrass beef skewers
— Drizzle over a sweet potato broccoli grain bowl (page 96)
— Massage into a kale salad with roasted sweet potatoes and sesame seeds on top
— Drizzle over sautéed broccoli and sprinkle with sesame seeds

Baked sweet potatoes with sesame ginger sauce

This recipe is inspired by chef Lucas Sin's famous Instagram post about freezing sweet potatoes (covered by Elazar Sontag in *Eater*). You can of course bake them using your favorite method, but I'm pretty sure this one is about to become your go-to. By freezing sweet potatoes and then baking them right from frozen, they turn out extra sweet and creamy. This method works particularly well for purple sweet potatoes, but you can also use it for other varieties.

———

⏱ **5+ MIN**
◔ 15+ MIN
◕ 30+ MIN

2 to 4 servings

2 purple sweet potatoes
Extra-virgin olive oil, for coating
Salt
Freshly ground black pepper
⅓ cup [80 g] sesame ginger sauce (page 191)
½ cup [30 g] sliced green onions
1 hot pepper, thinly sliced
2 tsp sesame seeds

Place the sweet potatoes in the freezer the day before you plan to bake them.

When you're ready to bake, preheat the oven to 350°F [180°C]. Place the frozen potatoes on a parchment-lined sheet pan, leaving room between them. Coat in a thin layer of oil and sprinkle with salt and pepper, as needed.

Bake for about 1½ hours, until the juices clinging to the skin are caramelized and the sweet potatoes are easily pierced with a fork. Some of the leaked goo will be burnt (leave that behind on the parchment), but if any is pooling and lightly caramelized, roll the sweet potato around in it to coat.

Split the potatoes open and top each one with the sesame ginger sauce, green onions, hot pepper, and sesame seeds and serve with a spoon.

Cold soba noodles

Silken is my favorite state of tofu. I love to invert it onto a plate, drizzle it with sesame ginger sauce, sprinkle on some green onions, and eat it with a spoon. But when I'm feeling a little more ambitious, I like to add big blocks to noodle salads like this one. Look for "firm silken tofu" for this recipe, which will hold its shape more than soft silken. Just don't confuse it with "firm tofu" here, which has a much firmer texture than we are after.

⏱ 5+ MIN
◔ **15+ MIN**
ⓘ 30+ MIN

4 servings as a main

8 oz [225 g] soba noodles
1⅓ cups [320 g] sesame ginger sauce (page 191)
Rice wine vinegar, for thinning
One 12.3 oz [350 g] package firm silken tofu
2 bell peppers, very thinly sliced
½ English cucumber, very thinly sliced
4 radishes, very thinly sliced
1 small bunch fresh basil
⅓ cup [20 g] sliced green onions
2 Tbsp sesame seeds
4 lime wedges

Boil the soba noodles according to the package instructions, then rinse them under cold water and drain well. Place the soba noodles in a large mixing bowl and top with ⅔ cup [155 g] of the sesame ginger sauce. Toss together well to coat very evenly and add more water or vinegar to thin it out and add a bit more acidity. Divide the noodles among 4 bowls.

Pat the silken tofu dry and cut the brick into 4 big cubes. Place one tofu cube in each bowl. Top each bowl with bell pepper, cucumber, and more sauce (2 to 3 Tbsp per bowl). Garnish with radishes, basil, green onions, sesame seeds, and lime wedges, and serve (squeeze the lime on at the last minute).

Make-ahead instructions
You can prep and assemble everything in individual takeout containers or bowls the day before, with the sauce on the side, and then pour the sauce on when you're ready.

Other components you can use
Use miso sweet potatoes (page 93) in place of some of the veggies, or add a little lemongrass beef (page 127).

Spring rolls

Spring rolls are a fun opportunity to get creative with vegetables and herbs. Shiso leaves, bean sprouts, tiny cooked shrimp—the sky's the limit! See substitutions for more ideas. Just try to stick to light and aromatic flavors, which will go wonderfully with the rich sesame dipping sauce.

———————

⏱ 5+ MIN
⊖ 15+ MIN
ⓘ **30+ MIN**

16 large or 22 small spring rolls

2½ oz [70 g] rice vermicelli (aka rice sticks)
1 tsp sesame oil
16 large or 22 small round rice papers (aka spring roll wrappers)
¾ cup [30 g] packed fresh cilantro leaves and small stems
1⅓ cups [20 g] packed fresh basil and/or mint leaves
2 carrots, julienned
1 bell pepper, julienned
1 small head red leaf lettuce, thinly sliced
⅓ English cucumber, julienned
1 cup [230 g] sesame ginger sauce (page 191)
Lime wedges, for serving

Boil the rice vermicelli according to the package directions until it's al dente. Rinse under cold water, shake well, chop coarsely, and toss in the sesame oil.

Place all of the ingredients within reach for easy assembly. Find a bowl that will fit the width of a rice paper, fill it with cold water, and place it next to a cutting board at your assembly station.

Dip one sheet of rice paper in the bowl of water, remove immediately, and place on the cutting board. It will soften after about 30 seconds.

Place a small amount of cilantro, basil, carrot, bell pepper, lettuce, cucumber, and cooked vermicelli in a log in the center of the paper. Fold the sides in, then fold up the bottom, and roll it up tightly (but not so tightly that the wrapper rips). Repeat with the remaining ingredients.

Serve with the sesame ginger sauce and lime wedges.

Recipe note
It's very important to follow the rice paper hydration instructions in the recipe. If you don't, your rice paper will be impossible to work with. You can only easily move it to the cutting board while it's still stiff, and it will soften with the residual moisture as it sits on the board. If you try to move it around once it's already softened, it will stick to itself.

Make-ahead instructions
Spring rolls can be made a day ahead and will keep in the refrigerator covered in plastic wrap. Make sure they're not touching each other or they may stick together. Alternatively, you can prep the fillings a day ahead and assemble the day of.

Substitutions
You can also replace some of the filling with tiny sautéed shrimp, perilla/shiso leaves, bean sprouts, shredded red cabbage, julienned green onion, sliced mango, sliced avocado, and/or julienned jalapeño.

Other components you can use
The lemongrass beef on page 127 works great here in place of some of the produce (slice it into smaller strips). You can also include a small amount of pickled mango (page 227) if you're looking for something sweet and tart to add.

Tzatziki

There are herby yogurt sauces all over the Mediterranean and Middle East, many with similar names. For instance, jajik in Iraq, cacik in Turkey, and (most well-known in the US) tzatziki in Greece. Whatever you're calling it, and wherever you are, the basic idea is the same: strain some yogurt and flavor it with herbs and/or cucumber. The herbs can be any variety of dill, mint, cilantro, or parsley—use whatever combination speaks to you, or whatever you've got in the fridge.

————

Makes 3 cups [695 g], enough to make all 3 recipes in this section

1½ cups [360 g] fat-free Greek yogurt
1½ cups [225 g] grated, wrung-out cucumber (from about 1 English cucumber)
3 Tbsp extra-virgin olive oil
3 Tbsp lemon juice
2 garlic cloves, crushed through a press
¾ tsp salt
½ tsp freshly ground black pepper
⅓ cup [15 g] chopped fresh dill, mint, cilantro, and/or parsley

In a medium mixing bowl, stir together the yogurt, cucumber, oil, lemon juice, garlic, salt, and pepper. Once combined, carefully fold in the herbs, just until evenly distributed.

Recipe note
You can use any combination of dill, mint, cilantro, and/or parsley, but it's best to choose at least 2. You can even substitute basil.

Storage
Tzatziki lasts for about 5 days in the fridge. It will last for at least 3 months in the freezer, but its texture will be affected, so you should only use it for cooking and not as a dip.

Store-bought alternatives
Some supermarkets sell tzatziki, which you can buy and use in any of the recipes in this section.

Pairing notes
Use tzatziki with any food that needs creaminess, herby flavor, and a little acidity. It goes particularly well with chicken, zesty spring vegetables, anything oniony—and as a dip with flatbread.

Ways to use:
— As a dip for pita and crudités (page 200)
— With za'atar chickpeas with yellow rice (page 202)
— For tzatziki fried chicken (page 204)
— Use to top mujadara (page 90)
— Serve with butter-basted lamb chops (page 228)
— Make souvlaki and thick-cut fries, and serve with tzatziki on the side
— Serve with Greek keftedes

Tzatziki with pita and crudités

This dish yields all sorts of aesthetic experiences. If you're having guests over, serve it in a little bowl surrounded by a rainbow array of nicely cut crudités and bread. If you're making a work lunch, pack up a bento with all your favorites in little compartments. Or if you're having a midnight snack all to yourself, peel a carrot to use as a trowel, and double-dip away.

⏱ **5+ MIN**
🕒 15+ MIN
🕦 30+ MIN

Place a bowl of tzatziki in the middle of a serving board. Slice raw veggies into dippable pieces, then arrange them around the bowl of dip with the pita and enjoy.

Tzatziki (page 199)
Carrots, radishes, celery, snap
    peas, and/or red peppers
Pita

Other components you can use
Crudités go great with the creamy Caesar dressing on page 155, the cilantro lime dressing on page 147, and the garlicky hummus on page 64.

Za'atar chickpeas with yellow rice

While often referred to as a dip, tzatziki also works great as a sauce. Serve it with mujadara (page 90), a grain bowl, or try this herby yellow rice and chickpea dish.

─────────

⏱ 5+ MIN
◔ **15+ MIN**
ⓘ 30+ MIN

4 to 6 servings

For the yellow rice:
1 cup [200 g] long-grain rice
1¼ cups [295 g] water, plus more
 for rinsing
2 Tbsp unsalted butter or
 extra-virgin olive oil
1 tsp ground turmeric
½ tsp salt

For the chickpeas:
¼ cup [30 g] za'atar
2 Tbsp extra-virgin olive oil
1 garlic clove, crushed through
 a press
½ tsp salt
Two 15 oz [425 g] cans chickpeas,
 drained and rinsed

To serve:
1¼ cups [300 g] tzatziki
 (page 199)
5 radishes, thinly sliced
¼ cup [10 g] chopped fresh dill,
 mint, cilantro, or parsley
Lemon wedges, for serving

Preheat the oven to 425°F [220°C].

To make the yellow rice, place the rice in a small saucepan. Cover with some cold water, swish around well, and drain. Add the rice back to the saucepan along with the water, butter, turmeric, and salt. Place over medium-high heat and bring to a simmer. Once simmering, cover and lower the heat to low. Simmer for 15 minutes without peeking or stirring. After 15 minutes, remove the saucepan from the heat but do not remove the lid, and let it rest for 10 to 25 more minutes.

Meanwhile, to make the chickpeas, stir together the za'atar, olive oil, garlic, and salt in a small mixing bowl. Place the chickpeas on a rimmed sheet pan. Top with the za'atar mixture and mix together using your hands, until the chickpeas are evenly coated. Roast for about 20 minutes, until a little crispy.

To serve, once the rice has rested, remove the lid and fluff with a fork. Place the rice in a serving bowl, top with a couple spoonfuls of the tzatziki, then the chickpeas, a few more spoonfuls of tzatziki, the radishes, and the chopped herbs. Serve immediately with lemon wedges and more tzatziki at the table.

Other components you can use
Try serving this with za'atar cauliflower (page 37) on the side.

Tzatziki fried chicken

The best fried chicken is made by marinating chicken pieces in buttermilk, dredging in flour, and moving them straight to the fryer. For a twist, I've replaced the buttermilk with tzatziki, but kept the same technique, which gets you a similar texture with a lovely herby cucumber flavor. This dish is best enjoyed immediately after it's made rather than stored ahead of time.

_____

⏱ 5+ MIN
⊖ 15+ MIN
ⓘ **30+ MIN**

3 servings

2 lb [910 g] chicken drumsticks (about 6)
1¼ tsp salt
⅔ cup [160 g] tzatziki (page 199), plus more for serving
Neutral oil, for deep-frying (such as canola)
1¼ cups [160 g] all-purpose flour

Place the chicken in a large bowl, sprinkle evenly with the salt, and top with the tzatziki. Use your hands to evenly coat the chicken, cover, and let it marinate in the fridge for at least 30 minutes, or for up to 1 day.

Once you're ready to fry, set up a safe fry station at your stove: Set a heavy pot on a back burner in a spot where it can't be knocked over, and fill it with 1 to 2 in [2.5 to 5 cm] of oil, leaving room at the top so it doesn't bubble over. Set over medium-low heat and clip a fry thermometer to the side of the pot. It's ready once it reaches 365°F [185°C].

Place the flour on a large plate. Lift a couple pieces of chicken out of the bowl (do not wipe away the marinade) and place on the plate with the flour. Flip them around a few times to coat evenly in flour, and set aside. Repeat with the remaining pieces.

Once your pieces are all dredged and the oil is hot, lower 3 of them into the oil. Increase the heat to high for a couple minutes and adjust so it maintains 330°F [160°C]. Let the chicken fry low and slow for about 15 minutes, flipping once halfway through. Keep an eye on the heat and adjust if it gets too high or low. The chicken is done once its internal temperature is 165°F [74°C].

Transfer to a wire rack–lined sheet pan, let the oil get to temperature again, and repeat with the second batch. Enjoy with more tzatziki on the side.

Fruits, compotes, and curds

This would typically be the part of the book where the savories end and the sweets begin. But since this book is a tad unconventional, it might not surprise you that the fruit section has several savory dishes as well. Here you'll find salads, pastries, cakes, and even lamb chops. Fruit brings an important sweet acidity to both dinner and dessert, and several of the components in this section can be used in either.

But cooking with fruit poses one important problem: While you can find many vegetables year-round, fruit tends to be much more tied to a particular season. Here's a quick cheat sheet for this section's components:

summer	cherry compote, macerated stone fruit or berries, roasted grapes
fall	mulled wine pears, roasted grapes
winter	mulled wine pears
spring	mulled wine pears, strawberry rhubarb compote
anytime	cinnamon apples, orange supremes, passion fruit curd, pickled mango, cherry compote made with frozen cherries

The beauty of processing fruit to be made into a component: You can easily freeze most of these components for later. So if you plan ahead, you can have anything any time of the year. I've also included some store-bought substitutes for certain components for maximum flexibility.

Cinnamon apples

These cinnamon apples add a little apple pie flavor to anything. Any crisp-tart apple variety that holds its shape when cooked will work great here (for instance, Pink Ladies, Honeycrisp, and Cosmic Crisp are a few of my favorites, and Granny Smiths are a reliable standard).

———————

Makes 5 to 6 cups [1 kg] cooked, enough to make any 1 recipe from this section

5 large or 8 medium apples (1 kg sliced)
½ cup [100 g] brown sugar
2½ tsp ground cinnamon

Peel, core, and slice the apples into ½ in [13 mm] thick wedges, and place in a microwave-safe bowl. Add the brown sugar and cinnamon and toss together. Let sit for about 5 minutes.

Microwave uncovered for about 8 minutes (depending on your microwave), stirring every 2 minutes or so. Stop once the apples have shrunk down and softened, but before they become mushy. Cool completely before filling pastries, or use warm as a breakfast topping.

Recipe note
If you don't want to make a whole batch, a good rule of thumb is to use about 1½ Tbsp brown sugar and about ½ tsp ground cinnamon per large apple (or 1 Tbsp brown sugar and about ¼ tsp ground cinnamon per medium apple). The cooking time will vary depending on how you scale up or down.

Storage
Store microwaved cinnamon apples in the fridge for up to 4 days. Don't worry about these apples oxidizing—they're covered in cinnamon, and no one will ever notice if they turn a little brown. Or store in the freezer for at least 3 months in a tightly sealed container.

Ways to use:
— With apple cinnamon oatmeal (page 210)
— Spooned over Thai tea ice cream (page 212)
— In apple cream puffs with cinnamon craquelin (page 214)
— Serve atop the miso sweet potato caramel brownies on page 98 along with a scoop of ice cream
— Use that last little bit of ricotta with your apples for a lovely snack
— Make an easy puff pastry tartlet (page 246)
— Add a tiny bit of apple cider vinegar for some acidity, then garnish some pork chops

— Fry some latkes and serve with cinnamon apples and sour cream
— Top Greek yogurt with cinnamon apples and your favorite granola

Apple cinnamon oatmeal

Porridge is my absolute favorite thing to eat for breakfast, although I'm fully aware that it has a bit of a reputation for being bland and uninspired. But as we fans can attest, it doesn't need to be that way. When perfectly executed, it's never stodgy or gloopy, always creamy and silky. The key to this wonderful texture? Using way more liquid than the side of the box tells you to.

⏱ **5+ MIN**
◔ 15+ MIN
ⓘ 30+ MIN

4 servings

2 cups [200 g] old-fashioned
   rolled oats
1 qt [960 g] milk
1 qt [940 g] water, plus more as
   needed
½ tsp salt
**1 batch cinnamon apples
   (page 209)**

Place the oats, milk, water, and salt in a large saucepan or medium stockpot. Stir together and set over medium heat. Give it a stir every few minutes as it comes to a simmer.

Once simmering, lower the heat to medium or medium-low. Maintain a simmer for 15 to 20 minutes, stirring occasionally and leaving it uncovered, until the oatmeal softens and the surrounding liquid thickens. In the beginning, it will be watery, but as the oat starches burst, the bubbles will become bigger and more sluggish. It should end up very creamy and pourable; if it starts to thicken too much from evaporation, add more water a couple tablespoons at a time. If it's too thin, let it cook for a few minutes longer to reduce down to your desired consistency. Serve with apples spooned on top.

Recipe note
If your pan is narrow, it might take longer for the liquid to reduce down and thicken. If it is extremely wide, you might need to add a little more liquid as it cooks.

Make-ahead instructions
Oatmeal will keep in the fridge for 3 to 4 days, or the freezer for at least 3 months. It will thicken more as it cools, so you should stir in a little more liquid before reheating.

Other components you can use
Top your oatmeal with cherry compote (page 259), macerated stone fruit or berries (page 251), mulled wine pears (page 243), or strawberry rhubarb compote (page 269).

Warm apples with Thai tea ice cream

Once every week or so in the summer, I replace my morning cup of coffee with a big glass of Thai iced tea. The bright orange color, vanilla scent, and sweetened condensed milk are intensely refreshing, and all work similarly wonderfully in an ice cream (especially a no-churn ice cream like this one, which relies on sweetened condensed milk for its texture). I love topping ice cream with fruit compotes, and apples go beautifully with the warm notes of Thai iced tea. This recipe doesn't require much active time, but it does require a couple days of waiting. But not to fear! If you need ice cream right now, simply buy a carton of vanilla and top it with warm cinnamon apples.

⏱ 5+ MIN

◔ **15+ MIN**

ⓘ 30+ MIN

8 servings

3 Tbsp vodka

1 Tbsp Thai tea mix for the vodka,
   1 Tbsp for the whipping cream

2 cups [460 g] heavy whipping
   cream

One 14 oz [395 g] can sweetened
   condensed milk

**1 batch cinnamon apples
   (page 209), warmed in the
   microwave**

½ cup [60 g] chopped salted
   roasted cashews

Make-ahead instructions
The ice cream will keep tightly sealed in the freezer for at least three months.

Other components you can use
Macerated nectarines or peaches (page 251) also work great here in place of the apples—add a few torn basil leaves for something special.

Place the vodka in a sealable container and stir in 1 Tbsp of the Thai tea mix. Cover and let sit at room temperature for at least 12 hours.

Meanwhile, place the heavy whipping cream in a microwave-safe container and stir in the remaining 1 Tbsp of the Thai tea mix. Microwave for about 3 minutes, stirring once halfway through, just until it's hot but not simmering (keep a close eye on it and don't let it boil). Move to the fridge for at least 12 hours.

The next day, strain the infused vodka through a fine-mesh sieve into a small bowl. Press against the sieve to wring out the leaves, and measure out 2 Tbsp of vodka. Discard the leaves and set the infused vodka aside.

Strain the steeped heavy whipping cream through the sieve into the bowl of a stand mixer (or in a mixing bowl if whisking by hand). Push the leaves against the sieve to wring them out, then discard the leaves. Beat the whipping cream to stiff peaks (slow down toward the end—do not overbeat, or it will turn into butter).

Add half of the sweetened condensed milk to the whipped cream and gently fold together with a spatula. Add the rest of the sweetened condensed milk and the infused vodka and gently fold together until well combined.

Transfer to a loaf pan or sealable container, cover, and freeze overnight until completely set. Serve a scoop of the ice cream with a scoop of the apples and a sprinkling of the chopped cashews.

Apple cream puffs with cinnamon craquelin

⏱ 5+ MIN
⊖ 15+ MIN
ⓘ **30+ MIN**

About 15 cream puffs

For the cinnamon craquelin:
⅔ cup [85 g] all-purpose flour
¼ cup plus 3 Tbsp [85 g] brown
  sugar
6 Tbsp [85 g] unsalted butter,
  at room temperature
1 tsp ground cinnamon
Pinch of salt

For the choux:
1 cup [235 g] water
¼ cup [55 g] unsalted butter
2 tsp granulated sugar
½ tsp salt
1¼ cups [165 g] all-purpose flour
4 large eggs, cracked into a liquid
  measuring cup

For the filling:
2 cups [460 g] heavy whipping
  cream
2 Tbsp granulated sugar
**1 batch cinnamon apples
  (page 209), cooled and strained**

Craquelin has two jobs: First, it creates a crumbly-crisp texture on top of each choux bun, and second, it helps each bun rise evenly. Here, it also adds some extra cinnamon-sugar flavor. These choux buns are best made up to a few hours before you plan to serve them, and it's best to assemble them at the last minute.

———

To make the craquelin, in the bowl of a stand mixer fitted with the paddle attachment, combine the flour, brown sugar, butter, cinnamon, and salt. Beat on low speed, just until it forms a smooth dough.

Dump the dough onto a sheet of parchment paper and pat it into a rectangle. Place another sheet of parchment on top and roll the whole thing out to about ¹⁄₁₆ in [1 to 2 mm] thick. Set on a level surface in the freezer for 1 hour.

To make the choux, preheat the oven to 400°F [205°C].

In a small saucepan over medium-high heat, combine the water, butter, granulated sugar, and salt and bring to a simmer. Once the butter melts and the water is simmering, immediately add the flour and remove from the heat. Stir together until it forms a lump-free ball, then transfer it to the bowl of a stand mixer fitted with the paddle attachment. Mix on medium-low speed for about 30 seconds.

Add the first egg with the mixer running on medium-low speed. Once the dough smooths out completely (30 to 45 seconds), continue the process with the rest of the eggs, waiting for each one to fully incorporate before adding the next. The pastry should drop from the top of the paddle in a V shape (see photo on page 217). Transfer the mixture to a large piping bag.

Line two sheet pans with parchment paper. Cut the tip of the piping bag to leave a ¾ in [19 mm] opening. Pipe 2½ in [6 cm] diameter circles, about 1 in [25 mm] tall, with a generous space between each.

Place the frozen craquelin sheet on the counter. Working quickly, stamp out enough 2½ in [6 cm] rounds to top your buns, and place a disc of craquelin on each one, pressing down the top slightly to flatten out any ridges in the choux. If the craquelin sheet starts to soften, re-freeze it so you can work with it.   **cont'd**

Bake for 15 minutes at 400°F [205°C], then lower the temperature to 350°F [180°C] and bake for about 20 more minutes, until golden brown. Let them cool at room temperature for at least 15 minutes, then slice them in half horizontally.

To make the filling, in the bowl of a stand mixer fitted with the whisk attachment, combine the whipping cream and granulated sugar and beat on medium speed for about 2½ minutes. As soon as it reaches medium-stiff peaks, stop whipping. Transfer the filling to a piping bag fitted with a star tip or grab a spoon for dolloping.

Pipe whipped cream onto the bottom of each choux bun. Top with a little scoop of apples, then top with more whipped cream and the bun lid.

Make-ahead instructions
The buns are best made up to a few hours before you plan to serve them. Do not cover the choux buns or they may become soggy. If they soften, pop them back in the oven for a couple minutes. You can prep the apples up to 4 days ahead and freeze the craquelin up to 2 weeks ahead of time.

Other components you can use
These are delicious with a smaller amount of cherry compote (page 259) or strawberry rhubarb compote (page 269) in place of the apples.

Roasted grapes

Fresh grapes are just wonderful, but they don't freeze and thaw well, they only last in the fridge for a week or so, and they're not so easy to bake with due to their high moisture content. Roasting is the solution for all grape-related problems. Make a big batch, freeze whatever you don't want to use right away, and thaw whenever.

———————

Makes about 1¾ cups [365 g], enough to make all 3 recipes in this section

5 cups [800 g] black or red grapes, from 1 large bunch
1 tsp neutral oil (such as avocado or canola)
¼ tsp salt

Preheat the oven to 350°F [180°C].

If you have any very large grapes, slice them in half. Smaller or medium grapes should be left whole. Place them on a rimmed sheet pan, coat in a thin layer of oil, sprinkle evenly with the salt, and spread them out into an even layer. Flip any face-down grapes so they're cut-side up.

Roast for about 35 minutes for smaller grapes, 60 minutes for larger grapes. They should shrink down significantly, and their bright purple juices should be a little syrupy but not burnt.

Remove from the sheet pan, syrup and all.

Storage
Roasted grapes will keep in the refrigerator for up to 5 days. They will last in the freezer for at least 3 months with no loss of quality, so immediately freeze any ones you don't plan to use in the first couple days. Freeze in small containers so that you can thaw just what you need. Thaw frozen roasted grapes in the refrigerator overnight or in the microwave at a low wattage.

Store-bought alternatives
Roasted grapes can be used in a very wide variety of recipes, so it's hard to give a blanket alternative. But note that they tend to add a little tart sweetness to anything. Grape jelly is a great alternative when you want the flavor but not the texture. Dried cranberries work well in place of roasted grapes in salads, especially alongside something like orange supremes (page 235) or grapefruit supremes, which have a similar texture.

Ways to use:
— On cashew butter toast (page 220)
— In incognito olive salad (page 222)
— For lemon grape poppy cake (page 224)
— Replace some or all of the blood oranges in the well-red chopped salad (page 34)
— Top some labneh (page 30) with roasted grapes and balsamic glaze
— Put them in a little bowl on a charcuterie board; roasted grapes serve a similar purpose to quince paste or pickled figs—something tangy and sweet to go with cheese, nuts, and cured meats
— Spread soft cheese (such as chèvre, Boursin, slices of Brie, etc.) on toast (dark rye works particularly well) and top with roasted grapes, then sprinkle with a little dried or fresh thyme
— Top ice cream with roasted grapes, hot fudge, and toasted peanuts

Cashew butter grape toast

I love using roasted grapes as if they're grape jam, as in this version of a cashew butter and jelly sandwich. You can even assemble it as a classic PB&J with the crusts cut off; the roasted grapes elevate a lunchbox favorite to a snack worthy of high tea.

———

⏱ **5+ MIN**
⊖ 15+ MIN
ⓘ 30+ MIN

Sliced multigrain bread
Cashew butter
Roasted grapes (page 219)
Sea salt

Toast enough pieces of bread to make as many open-faced sandwiches as you'd like.

Spread cashew butter on each piece of toast, top with roasted grapes and sea salt, and enjoy.

Incognito olive salad

Roasted grapes and wrinkly black olives look indistinguishable, but these two ingredients couldn't taste more different, so placing them together in a salad is a fun change of pace. My typical salad-eating method is to aim for a perfect bite of every ingredient every time, but that's not possible when these two are involved. You've just got to surrender to fate and prepare yourself for sweet, savory, or a little bit of both with every bite.

⏱ 5+ MIN
◔ **15+ MIN**
ⓘ 30+ MIN

6 servings

3 thick slices rye bread
1 Tbsp extra-virgin olive oil
Salt
10 oz [285 g] bag spinach
5 Tbsp [75 g] actually good vinaigrette (page 139), made with balsamic vinegar
3 oz [80 g] Bulgarian sheep's milk cheese
⅔ cup [140 g] roasted grapes (page 219)
¼ cup [30 g] pitted black oil-cured olives
3 sprigs fresh thyme

Preheat the oven to 350°F [180°C].

Cut the bread into ¾ in [19 mm] cubes and place on a rimmed sheet pan. Drizzle with the olive oil and toss to coat evenly. Sprinkle with a pinch of salt. Bake for about 15 minutes, until crunchy. Let the croutons cool on the pan while you assemble the salad.

Place the spinach in a salad bowl. Drizzle lightly with 4 Tbsp [60 g] of the vinaigrette and toss to coat. Top with the cooled croutons, cheese, grapes, and black olives. Strip the thyme leaves from the stems as you sprinkle them over the salad. Drizzle with the remaining 1 Tbsp of vinaigrette. Break off a piece of the cheese hunk with each serving.

Make-ahead instructions
Mix the dressing up to 2 weeks ahead. Find the freshest bag of spinach you can and keep the bag closed until you plan to use it. Make the croutons up to 3 weeks ahead and store them in the freezer (thaw uncovered on a plate for a few minutes at room temperature, or refresh them in a toaster oven at 350°F [180°C] for a few minutes if they taste stale after thawing). If you don't want to eat the whole salad at once, just use as much of each ingredient as you need and store the rest in the fridge.

Substitutions
Castelvetrano olives work in place of the black olives, especially if you're not a huge olive fan. They're very mild and citrusy. You can also substitute Greek feta in place of Bulgarian sheep's milk cheese. If you don't have fresh thyme on hand, shake up the dressing with a couple pinches of dried thyme. Also feel free to use a bolder dressing, like the creamy Caesar on page 155.

Lemon grape poppy cake

While grapes are way too high-moisture for most baking projects, roasting them changes everything. About half of their moisture gets cooked off, opening the door to so many possibilities, like this delicious cake.

———

⏱ 5+ MIN
⊖ 15+ MIN
ⓘ **30+ MIN**

One 8 by 4 in [20 by 10 cm] cake

For the cake:
Butter, for greasing the pan
1⅔ cups [215 g] all-purpose flour
2 tsp baking powder
½ tsp salt
1 cup [200 g] granulated sugar
¾ cup [180 g] buttermilk
½ cup [105 g] neutral oil, plus more for greasing the pan (optional)
3 large eggs
1 Tbsp lemon zest, plus more for garnish
¼ cup [35 g] poppy seeds, plus more for garnish
⅔ cup [140 g] strained roasted grapes (page 219)

For the glaze:
1½ Tbsp pan juices from roasted grapes
½ cup [60 g] powdered sugar

To make the cake, preheat the oven to 350°F [180°C]. Butter or oil an 8 by 4 in [20 by 10 cm] loaf pan and line it with a parchment sling.

In a medium mixing bowl, whisk together the flour, baking powder, and salt.

In another medium mixing bowl, whisk together the granulated sugar, buttermilk, oil, eggs, lemon zest, and poppy seeds. Pour the wet ingredients over the dry ingredients and give it a couple folds. Add the strained grapes and continue folding until there are no dry flour pockets. Do not overmix.

Transfer to the prepared pan and smooth out the top. Bake for about 1 hour, until a toothpick inserted into the center comes out clean. Loosen the edges with a knife and remove from the pan to a wire rack. Let it cool completely (at least 1 hour) before glazing or slicing.

To make the glaze, in a small mixing bowl, whisk together the pan juices and powdered sugar until the consistency is right for drizzling. Once the cake cools, glaze it and sprinkle on more lemon zest and poppy seeds.

Make-ahead instructions
This cake can be made a day ahead of time for guests—as long as you don't slice into it, it will not stale in the first day. For longer-term storage for leftovers, slice and freeze.

Substitutions
Replace the grapes with 1 cup [130 g] of blueberries for a lemon poppy blueberry cake. Purée about 2 Tbsp of blueberries with ½ cup [60 g] of powdered sugar for the glaze.

Pickled mango

Amba is a Middle Eastern style of pickled underripe mango—ripe mangoes are super sweet, but underripe ones are nicely astringent, which works great as an acidic pickle. Underripe mangoes should be firm, but not rock-hard, and when you cut into them, they should be a little rubbery rather than crunchy or juicy. On the other hand, if you only have ripe mangoes, they will work here as long as they are not yet mushy (for ripe mangoes, do not simmer them, and simply pour the hot liquid over them in their containers).

————

Makes 2 pints [980 g], enough to make all 3 recipes in this section

2 large or 3 medium underripe
  green mangoes
¾ cup [175 g] water
¾ cup [175 g] apple cider vinegar
2 Tbsp lemon juice
1 Tbsp yellow curry powder
2 tsp sugar
2 tsp salt
½ tsp red pepper flakes

Peel and slice the mangoes into matchsticks and place in a saucepan. Add the water, vinegar, lemon juice, curry powder, sugar, salt, and red pepper flakes and set over medium-high heat. As soon as it reaches a low boil, cover, lower the heat to low, and simmer for about 5 minutes until the mangoes have softened.

Remove from the heat and pour into 2 pint jars to store in the refrigerator. Pickled mango is best after at least 1 day, but you can use it right away.

Storage
Pickled mango will keep for at least 1 week in the refrigerator and at least 3 months in the freezer with no loss of quality.

Store-bought alternatives
You can buy amba in most Middle Eastern markets.

Ways to use:
— With butter-basted lamb chops
  (page 228)
— In masgouf (page 230)
— For falafel crumble pita pocket
  (page 232)
— Add a little bit to spring rolls
  (page 196) for extra bite and
  sweetness
— Add some pickled mango next
  time you make ceviche
— Use instead of salsa next time
  you make tacos
— Add to a charcuterie board for
  something sweet and tangy
— Top a seared steak (see page 86)
  for some acidity and a pop
  of color

Butter-basted lamb chops with pickled mango

By cooking lamb chops at a moderate temperature in a lot of butter (rather than searing over high heat with a little oil), they'll cook to medium-rare without much fuss. While 6 Tbsp [85 g] of butter might sound like a lot, most of it doesn't end up in the final dish. Instead, the pool of butter sizzles up the sides of the lamb chops, giving them a super even sear and imparting a ton of flavor. This technique is slightly slower than searing or grilling, but once you get the heat right, you don't have to do much babysitting and can just flip them when they're ready, with minimal active time.

———————

⏱ **5+ MIN**
◔ 15+ MIN
◔ 30+ MIN

2 to 3 servings

1 lb 10 oz [730 g] lamb loin or rib chops (about 6)
1 tsp salt
2 tsp garlic powder (optional)
½ tsp freshly ground black pepper
6 Tbsp [85 g] unsalted butter
½ cup [100 g] pickled mango pieces, lifted out of their brine (page 227)

Sprinkle the lamb chops evenly with the salt, then the garlic powder, if using, and pepper and let sit while you get the pan ready (at least 2 minutes, ideally 5 to 15).

Place the butter in a large sauté pan or cast-iron skillet and set it over medium-high heat. Swirl the butter around as it melts. Once the butter melts completely, add the lamb chops (don't crowd the pan, and work in batches if necessary). Once the chops are rapidly sizzling, lower the heat to medium to maintain a moderate sizzle; adjust the heat as necessary to make sure the butter is always sizzling but does not burn. Let the chops sear for about 6 minutes on each side. They're done once they've browned and their internal temperature is 135°F [57°C].

Set on a serving plate, top with pickled mango, and enjoy.

Make-ahead instructions
Season the lamb right when you get it home from the market, cover, and refrigerate for up to 3 days. Pickle the mangoes ahead, and then cook the lamb at the last minute.

Other components you can use
Instead of amba, top the lamb chops with caramelized tomatoes (page 101), avocado tomatillo salsa verde (page 163), or tzatziki (page 199).

Masgouf

Masgouf is a classic Iraqi way of grilling fish. While fire-roasting is traditional, I bake a batch on a big sheet pan in the oven so that the top can caramelize. And while carp is the standard, I love using whole butterflied snapper or branzino.

⏱ 5+ MIN
◷ **15+ MIN**
ⓘ 30+ MIN

4 servings

¾ cup [150 g] strained pickled mango, plus more for serving, plus 1 Tbsp brine (page 227)
1½ cups [225 g] cherry tomatoes, halved
½ small red onion, thinly sliced
4 tsp yellow curry powder
¾ tsp salt
1 lb 5 oz [600 g] lean white fish, patted dry and cut into 4 fillets
1 Tbsp lemon juice

Preheat the oven to 500°F [260°C]. Lightly oil a rimmed sheet pan.

In a small bowl, combine the pickled mango, brine, cherry tomatoes, red onion, 2 tsp of the curry powder, and ¼ tsp of the salt. Toss together and set aside.

Place the fish on the sheet pan and season with the remaining ½ tsp of salt. Drizzle on the lemon juice and sprinkle evenly with the remaining 2 tsp of curry powder on both sides. Top with the tomato-mango mixture (leave behind any liquid). Roast for 12 to 15 minutes, until the tomatoes are blistered and charred and the fish is easily flaked with a fork. Serve with more amba, if desired.

Recipe note
You can use fillets here, but you can also use just about any lean white fish variety. Or go for whole, butterflied fish instead of fillets.

Make-ahead instructions
You can make the topping up to 1 day ahead (cover and refrigerate). Put everything together and roast at the last minute.

Falafel crumble pita pocket

Well, I've got good news and bad. First the bad news: To make good falafel, you've got to plan a day ahead, because using fresh, soaked chickpeas is absolutely essential. But here's the good news: Once your chickpeas have soaked, you can absolutely get away with skipping the deep fryer. Instead, simply spread falafel mix on a sheet pan, drizzle with olive oil, and bake it. There's a particular technique to it involving flipping everything in big sections instead of just mixing it all up, but this recipe has got you covered.

⏱ 5+ MIN
⊖ 15+ MIN
ⓘ **30+ MIN**

4 to 6 servings

For soaking:
3 qt [2.8 L] water
1½ cups [285 g] dried chickpeas
1 Tbsp baking soda

For the falafel:
4 garlic cloves
½ cup [20 g] packed fresh cilantro
  leaves
½ cup [20 g] packed fresh dill
  fronds
2 green onions
2 Tbsp water
1½ tsp ground cumin
1 tsp paprika
1 tsp freshly ground black pepper
1 tsp salt
½ tsp baking soda
3 Tbsp extra-virgin olive oil
Pickled mango (page 227),
  for serving
4 to 6 pita pockets
4 to 6 romaine leaves

To soak, place the water, chickpeas, and baking soda in a large container. Mix together, cover with plastic wrap, and let sit for 16 to 24 hours. The chickpeas are done soaking once their centers are completely hydrated.

Once your chickpeas have soaked, preheat the oven to 475°F [245°C].

To make the falafel, place the drained soaked chickpeas in a food processor with the garlic, cilantro, dill, green onions, water, cumin, paprika, pepper, salt, and baking soda. Blend until the chickpeas are the texture of fine couscous.

Drizzle 1 Tbsp of the olive oil on a rimmed sheet pan. Use your hands to evenly coat the surface. Sprinkle the falafel mix over the sheet pan in an even layer. Do not tamp it down, and leave it somewhat fluffy. Drizzle very evenly with the remaining 2 Tbsp of olive oil.

Bake for about 15 minutes on the first side, then use a spatula to flip the falafel in about 15 sections, breaking it up as little as possible. Bake again for about 15 minutes on the other side, until it's golden brown and very crunchy on the outside and fluffy and cooked through on the inside. Break it up into smaller crumbles and enjoy with pickled mango, pita, and romaine.

Make-ahead instructions
Falafel crumbles will keep for 4 to
5 days in the fridge.

Orange supremes

Most of an orange's flavor is concentrated in its zest, so I never miss an opportunity to add it back in when working with orange pieces. Before cutting oranges, first zest them, then supreme them, and then sprinkle a big pinch of that zest in with the supremes. If you've got some zest leftover, use it within a couple hours (for instance, add to a chicken dry-brine), or preserve it with some sugar using the suggestion following this recipe.

Makes 3⅓ cups [540 g] orange supremes, enough to make either the vegan double-chocolate orange tart or both the orange supremes with ricotta and the spinach salad

6 large or 10 medium oranges
1 tsp sugar

First, zest your oranges (avoid any white pith). Set the zest aside.

Use a paring knife to slice the top off one orange, then slice the bottom off. Rest the orange on the cutting board on one of the flat ends. Place the knife's edge right where the pith meets the flesh on top, and slice down at an angle to strip the skin away. Watch your fingers and do not cut toward them. Repeat until the orange is completely peeled.

Place the orange on its side and carefully slice along one membrane, then another membrane to release 1 segment. Pop out the segment into a resealable container and continue with the rest. Repeat with the other oranges.

Sprinkle the orange supremes with half of their zest and the sugar and gently toss together until coated evenly. Strain before using.

Recipe notes
Save some of the zest if you're making the vegan double-chocolate orange tart on page 240. Or preserve it in sugar: Combine the remaining half of the orange zest with 1 cup [200 g] sugar to make orange sugar. Place on a plate or quarter sheet pan and rub it between your fingers until the zest is evenly distributed. Shake it out into an even layer and leave it to dry at room temperature for 2 to 12 hours (depending on the climate). Once it's crusty, rub the sugar between your fingers to break up any clumps and let it sit out for another few hours. Once it's completely dried out, store it in a sealed container for a few weeks to use in baking, cocktails, etc.

Storage
Orange supremes will keep for 2 to 3 days in the fridge. Whole oranges will keep for much longer, so only prep as many as you'll use in a few days.

Ways to use:
— With a little scoop of ricotta (page 236)
— With spinach salad (page 238)
— For vegan double-chocolate orange tart (page 240)
— Flavor whipped cream with a little vanilla extract and top with orange supremes to make a dreamsicle fool (see page 270)
— Blood oranges are featured in the well-red chopped salad on page 34, but you can use any variety
— Make a simple composed salad with citrus supremes, pitted Castelvetrano olives, giant flakes of Pecorino Romano (use a vegetable peeler) and actually good vinaigrette (page 139)
— Add to your favorite fruit salad (top it instead of folding them in)

Orange supremes with ricotta

Many recipes ask you to use an odd amount of ricotta, leaving you with a few spoonfuls leftover. Instead of relegating that mostly empty tub to the back of the fridge, take it as an opportunity to make a delicious snack. The following can be made right in the container. Just top it with your favorite fruit, a little honey, and some nuts, and enjoy.

🕐 **5+ MIN**
⊖ 15+ MIN
ⓘ 30+ MIN

Ricotta
Orange supremes (page 235)
Honey
Ground pistachios or slivered
  almonds

Place a small scoop of ricotta in a small bowl or ramekin. Top with a few orange supremes, a drizzle of honey, and a sprinkle of ground pistachios or slivered almonds.

Other components you can use
Substitute the supremes with roasted grapes (page 219), macerated stone fruit (page 251) or apple slices, mulled wine pears (page 243), passion fruit curd (page 277), or fresh summer berries.

Spinach salad

This salad is super simple, but big on flavor. Orange supremes go great with any savory cheese, especially your favorite funky blue.

———————

⏱ 5+ MIN
⊖ **15+ MIN**
ⓘ 30+ MIN

6 servings

One 5 oz [140 g] bag baby spinach
**4 Tbsp [60 g] actually good
   vinaigrette (page 139)**
One 15 oz [425 g] can white beans
**1 cup [180 g] heaped orange
   supremes (page 235)**
1 cup [150 g] blue cheese crumbles
1 cup [100 g] coarsely chopped
   walnuts

Place the spinach in a salad bowl, then top with 2 Tbsp of the vinaigrette and toss together.

Top the salad with the beans, orange supremes, blue cheese, and walnuts, followed by the remaining 2 Tbsp of vinaigrette.

Make-ahead instructions
Make the dressing and store it in the fridge for a few days. Do not open the spinach bag until right before serving. Crumble the blue cheese, chop the walnuts, and supreme the oranges 1 to 2 days ahead.

Other components you can use
Try substituting mulled wine pears (page 243), roasted grapes (page 219), marinated beets (page 29), or macerated apricots (page 251) in place of some or all of the orange supremes. Or try the cilantro lime dressing (page 147) instead of the vinaigrette and feta in place of the blue cheese for a completely different flavor profile.

Vegan double-chocolate orange tart

A friend of mine went vegan in our first year of college. While browsing the dining hall junk food display, we were thrilled to discover that Oreos are entirely (and somewhat surprisingly) plant-based. Ever since, they're my favorite thing to use in a vegan cookie-crumb crust.

———

○ 5+ MIN
◔ 15+ MIN
ⓘ **30+ MIN**

6 to 8 servings

For the crust:
35 Oreos
3 Tbsp melted coconut oil
2 tsp water
¼ tsp salt

For the ganache:
⅔ cup [155 g] full-fat coconut milk
    (shaken before measuring)
1 cup [150 g] chopped 70% dark
    chocolate
1 tsp orange zest
Salt
**1 batch orange supremes
    (page 235)**
2 Tbsp orange marmalade
    (optional)

Preheat the oven to 350°F [180°C].

To make the crust, place the Oreos in a food processor fitted with the blade attachment. Blend until they're broken down into fine crumbs. Add the coconut oil, water, and salt. Blend until it's the consistency of wet sand. Dump the mixture into a 10 in [25 cm] tart shell and tamp it down so it covers the bottom and sides in an even, compact layer.

Bake for about 14 minutes, until it smells toasty and looks more set. Leave the crust in the tart shell as it cools and hardens.

To make the ganache, heat the coconut milk in the microwave just until steaming. Place the chopped chocolate, orange zest, and a pinch of salt in a medium mixing bowl. Pour the hot coconut milk over the chocolate and let it sit for 1 minute. Whisk the ganache together until completely smooth (do not reheat).

Pour the warm ganache into the baked crust and smooth out the top. Place it in the fridge and let it chill for at least 2 hours. Once set, arrange the orange supremes on top. Place the marmalade, if using, in a small bowl, microwave it until runny, and brush it over the orange slices. Serve immediately.

Make-ahead instructions
Bake the crust up to 1 day before filling, prep the orange supremes the day before, and then make the ganache and assemble at the last minute.

Other components you can use
Try cherry compote (page 259) or strained macerated strawberries (page 251) in place of the orange supremes.

Mulled wine pears

Conventional wisdom states that you should never cook with a wine that you wouldn't actually drink. But these mulled wine pears are so beautifully spiced, you can absolutely use the most mediocre wine you can find. The poaching liquid will transform into a fabulous spiced syrup when all is said and done.

————

Makes 7 poached pears [90 g each], enough to make either the mulled wine pears with mascarpone and streusel or both the puff pastry tartlets and spiced chocolate pear cake

7 semi-ripe firm Bosc pears
  (see recipe note)
1 bottle [750 ml] red wine
1 cup [200 g] sugar
1 scraped vanilla pod or 2 tsp
  vanilla bean paste
½ tsp ground cinnamon
1 whole star anise pod (optional)
5 cardamom pods (optional)

Recipe note
Semi-ripe firm pears are pears that have sat at room temperature for 1 to 2 days after bringing them home rock-hard from the supermarket. They shouldn't have much give, but should be a little juicy when you cut into one.

Storage
Use any pears floating above the surface within the first day or 2, then keep the fully submerged pears for up to 5 days. Or slice in half, submerge in syrup, and freeze in a tightly sealed container. Pears can be kept this way for at least 3 months with no loss of quality.

Store-bought alternatives
You can use canned pears in juice for any of this section's recipes, so long as they're high quality and not soggy. Make sure you strain them well so there isn't juice clinging to them.

Use a zucchini corer or a small melon baller to drill into each pear from the bottom, scooping out the seeds and any stony bits. After coring, peel the pears.

Place the pears in a small saucepan and add the wine, sugar, vanilla, cinnamon, star anise, if using, and cardamom, if using. Bring to a simmer, uncovered, over medium heat, keeping a very close eye on it. As soon as bubbles begin to break the surface, gradually lower the heat to low to maintain a bare simmer. Do not let it boil or your pears will turn to mush; tiny bubbles should break to the surface around the pears, almost like effervescence.

Simmer, uncovered, for about 30 minutes. Gently rotate the pears a couple times to make sure they're cooking evenly. They are done once you can easily insert a paring knife into the pear while still feeling a little resistance.

Transfer the pears with a slotted spoon to a container that snugly fits them.

Bring the poaching liquid back to a simmer over medium-high heat. Let it reduce down to ⅓ to ½ its original volume (to 1¼ to 1½ cups [350 to 425 g]; it takes about 20 minutes, but varies a lot based on the width of your pan). Pour the liquid over the pears and refrigerate until ready to use.

Ways to use:
— With mascarpone and streusel (page 244)
— On puff pastry tartlets (page 246)
— Baked into a spiced chocolate pear cake (page 248)
— With a little ricotta, honey, and pistachio (see page 236)
— Slice and toss into a spinach salad (page 238)
— Add to the well-red chopped salad (page 34)
— In place of the apples in apple cinnamon oatmeal (page 210)
— Sliced and served on a charcuterie board with blue cheese, prosciutto, and pecans
— Serve a hot poached pear with a scoop of ice cream, a drizzle of syrup, and cookie crumbles

Mulled wine pears with mascarpone and streusel

Streusel is normally crumbled onto batter and then baked, but I love baking up a big batch separately and crumbling it over fruit, ice cream, and the like. Streusel takes literally 5 minutes to whip up and pop in the oven, and you can store it in the freezer pretty much indefinitely, so it's great to have on hand for entertaining or late-night snacks. To bring this down to zero minutes of active time, simply crumble your favorite cookies instead.

———

⏱ **5+ MIN**
◔ 15+ MIN
◔ 30+ MIN

7 servings

For the streusel:
½ cup [65 g] all-purpose flour
⅓ cup [65 g] brown sugar
⅓ cup [35 g] old-fashioned
    rolled oats
¼ cup [55 g] cold unsalted butter,
    cut into small pieces
½ tsp ground cinnamon
Pinch of salt

For serving:
1½ cups [345 g] mascarpone
1 batch mulled wine pears
    (page 243) and their syrup

Preheat the oven to 350°F [180°C].

To make the streusel, place the flour, brown sugar, oats, butter, cinnamon, and salt in a small mixing bowl. Use your hands to work it together until it's well incorporated and clumpy.

Sprinkle the mixture onto a parchment-lined quarter sheet pan, breaking up any big clumps by rubbing them between your fingers. Bake for about 15 minutes, until golden brown. Let cool completely on the pan. Break up into clumps once it cools.

To serve, place little scoops of mascarpone in 7 small bowls. Top each with a pear, a drizzle of syrup, and some streusel.

Make-ahead instructions
Streusel can be made ahead and stored at room temperature for 4 to 5 days before staling slightly. For longer-term storage, tightly seal and freeze for a few weeks (do not thaw, and just use it right from the freezer).

Substitutions
You can use biscoff crumbles in place of streusel for a very quick shortcut. You can also use fresh summer berries in place of the mulled wine pears.

Other components you can use
Macerated stone fruit (page 251), cherry compote (page 259), cinnamon apples (page 209)

Puff pastry tartlets

I always keep puff pastry on hand in my freezer, which makes it easy to whip up little tartlets when I need a last-minute dessert. And if you've got poached pears tucked away in the fridge, these puff pastry tartlets are a cinch.

———————

⏱ 5+ MIN
◷ **15+ MIN**
◔ 30+ MIN

8 servings

4 oz [115 g] cream cheese, at room temperature
2 Tbsp mulled wine syrup (see page 243)
1 tsp ground cinnamon
12 oz [340 g] puff pastry, thawed in the refrigerator
1 large egg beaten with 1 tsp water
4 mulled wine pears (page 243), sliced in half

Preheat the oven to 430°F [220°C]. Line 2 rimmed sheet pans with parchment paper.

Whisk the cream cheese, syrup, and cinnamon together in a small mixing bowl until it's completely smoothed out.

If your puff pastry isn't already rolled out to ⅛ in [3 mm], roll it out on a lightly floured clean counter. Cut into 8 squares.

Place the squares of puff pastry on the sheet pans. Using a paring knife, cut a ¼ in [6 mm] border in one of the squares, leaving it attached at 2 opposite corners. You should end up with 2 V-shaped borders attached to a square base. Lift one of the Vs, and cross it over to the other side of the puff pastry base. Do the same with the other V, letting it rest on the other side of the base. Lightly brush underneath the strips with egg wash and repeat with the remaining squares.

Place a dollop of the cream cheese mixture in the center of each square, followed by a half pear each. Brush with more egg wash.

Bake for about 15 minutes, until puffed up and golden brown.

Make-ahead instructions
These are best made right before serving, but leftovers keep well in the fridge for a couple days. To make ahead, prep all your components and set your puff pastry on sheet pans in the fridge the day before.

Substitutions
While it won't have the same mulled wine flavor, you can use canned pears in this recipe.

Use a smaller amount of pear juice with a little sugar in place of the syrup, just until the cream cheese thins out slightly. Strain the pear slices well and fan them out over the cream cheese. You can also use fresh summer berries.

Other components you can use
In place of the pears, use strained cinnamon apples (page 209) or strained macerated stone fruit or berries (page 251).

Spiced chocolate pear cake

Cookbook author Zoë François's poached pear ginger cake inspired this chocolate pear loaf, with a wintry forest of pear stems poking out of the top, and a pink drizzle of poaching syrup glaze.

———

⏱ 5+ MIN
◔ 15+ MIN
ⓘ **30+ MIN**

6 big servings

For the cake:
1 cup [130 g] all-purpose flour
½ cup [40 g] cocoa powder
2 tsp ground cinnamon
1½ tsp baking powder
½ tsp ground cardamom
¾ cup [150 g] brown sugar
¼ cup [55 g] unsalted butter, melted, plus more for greasing the pan
¼ cup [55 g] canola oil
2 large eggs, at room temperature
1 tsp salt
⅔ cup [160 g] buttermilk, at room temperature
⅔ cup [85 g] finely chopped walnuts, plus more for sprinkling
3 whole mulled wine pears (page 243)

For the icing:
2 to 3 Tbsp mulled wine pear syrup (page 243)
1 cup [120 g] powdered sugar

To make the cake, preheat the oven to 350°F [180°C]. Butter a 9 by 5 in [23 by 13 cm] or 8 by 4 in [20 cm by 10 cm] loaf pan and line with a parchment sling.

In a medium mixing bowl, whisk (or sift) together the flour, cocoa powder, cinnamon, baking powder, and cardamom until lump-free. Set aside.

Place the brown sugar, melted butter, oil, eggs, and salt in another medium mixing bowl. Whisk together until combined. Add the buttermilk and whisk together until completely smooth.

Sprinkle the walnuts over the dry ingredients, then pour on the wet ingredients and stir together just until there are no lumps (do not overmix).

Pour the batter into the prepared loaf pan and smooth out the top. Submerge the pears in the batter, standing upright, evenly distributing them. To keep them from falling over, optionally place metal skewers through them horizontally so that the skewers rest on the pan.

Bake for about 60 minutes, until a toothpick inserted in a gap between 2 pears comes out clean. Let cool in the pan for about 15 minutes, then transfer to a wire rack to cool at room temperature.

To make the icing, while the cake cools, in a small mixing bowl, whisk together the syrup and powdered sugar. Drizzle the glaze onto the cooled cake and sprinkle with more walnuts.

Make-ahead instructions
This cake is best enjoyed the day it's made. You can store it in the refrigerator for about 1 day, but butter cakes tend to stale in the fridge, and the pears should not be left at room temperature. It's better to freeze any leftover slices (they will keep for weeks).

Substitutions
You can use canned pears here—just make sure you strain them very well and pat them dry. Use about 1 cup [150 g]. Gently fold them into the batter once the dry ingredients are almost completely incorporated. You can also use a 8 by 4 in [20 by 10 cm] pan, but it may take 5 to 10 minutes longer to cook through.

Macerated stone fruit or berries

A stone fruit is simply any summer fruit that has a hard pit at its center: cherries, apricots, plums, peaches, and so on. And while "berry" has a very specific botanical definition, recipes usually just intend anything with the actual word "berry" in its name. Anything from these two categories will macerate beautifully. Simply coat in sugar, wait for a while, and let their syrups gather. Whether you want to use the syrup depends on what you're making. It's either an opportunity to drive off some moisture, or something sweet to drizzle.

Makes 5 to 8 cups macerated fruit (check recipes for particular varieties and quantities)

7 to 9 cups (1 kg) pitted semi-ripe stone fruit or berries (see recipe notes)
½ cup [100 g] sugar

Prep your fruit (see recipe notes). Place the fruit in a large bowl or storage container and top with the sugar. Stir together until the sugar coats the fruit completely, refrigerate, and let sit for at least 15 minutes before using.

Recipe notes
Slice in half if your stone fruits are very small (for instance sugar plums), slice into wedges if your stone fruits are large, leave small berries whole, and slice strawberries. In general, 1 kg is about 8 cups of sliced strawberries or stone fruit (peach, nectarine, plum, apricot, etc.), 9 cups whole raspberries or blackberries, or 7 cups whole blueberries or halved apricots/small plums. If you want a smaller amount, you can cut the recipe in half to 3½ to 4½ cups [500 g] fruit and ¼ cup [50 g] sugar.

Storage
Macerated fruit keeps in the refrigerator for up to 5 days (discard sooner if you catch a whiff of alcohol).

Ways to use:
— For strawberry shortcakes (page 252)
— With pork chops with nectarine salsa (page 254)
— In Polish plum cake (page 256)
— Top a bowl of oatmeal (see page 210)
— Use in place of the pears and syrup in the puff pastry tartlets on page 246

— Top the mousse on page 260 with macerated fruit instead of cherries
— Serve the Thai tea ice cream on page 212 with macerated peaches or nectarines instead of apples
— Strain and top the vegan double-chocolate tart on page 240 in place of the oranges
— Swirl both fruit and syrup into yogurt
— Serve slices of pound cake with a scoop of macerated fruit
— Use as the fruit filling/topping on a pavlova (skip the syrup, or it will become soggy)

Strawberry shortcakes

To keep this recipe around 5 minutes of active time, skip the biscuit-making part and simply use canned biscuits. But if you've got a few extra minutes, give it a try. Since strawberry shortcakes tend to be a little on the sweet side, my favorites are always made with unsweetened buttermilk biscuits. The biscuit soaks up all the whipped cream and strawberry juices, and the combination turns out perfectly sweet.

⌚ **5+ MIN**
◔ 15+ MIN
ⓘ 30+ MIN

12 servings

For the biscuits:
2¾ cups [360 g] all-purpose flour, plus more for dusting
1½ Tbsp baking powder
1 tsp salt
8 Tbsp [115 g] cold unsalted butter
1¼ cups [300 g] cold buttermilk, plus more for brushing

For the toppings:
½ tsp freshly ground black pepper (optional)
8 cups [1 kg] strawberry slices, macerated with ½ cup [100 g] sugar (see page 251)
1 cup [240 g] heavy whipping cream

Preheat the oven to 445°F [230°C]. Line a sheet pan with parchment paper.

To make the biscuits, stir together the flour, baking powder, and salt in a medium mixing bowl. Cut the butter into tablespoons and add it to the flour mixture. Pinch the tablespoons of butter about 2 times per tablespoon, just to flatten them. There should be lots of butter chunks left. Add the buttermilk and stir together just until it forms a dough (do not overmix).

Dust a clean counter with flour, turn the biscuit dough onto the counter, sprinkle the top with flour, and roll it into a ½ in [13 mm] thick rectangle the size of a piece of letter-size paper. Fold like a tri-fold letter, roll out into another ½ in [13 mm] thick rectangle, fold again, and repeat one more time for a total of three rolls.

Move the dough to the prepared sheet pan and roll the dough out to a 9 by 6 in [23 by 15 cm] rectangle. Cut in half lengthwise, then into thirds in the other direction to make 6 squares. Slice diagonally to cut each square into 2 triangles, for a total of 12 pieces. Do not separate them. Brush the tops lightly with more buttermilk.

Bake the biscuits for about 20 minutes (they're done once they're golden brown, puffed up, and baked through).

To make the toppings, in a large mixing bowl, stir together the pepper, if using, and the macerated strawberries, and set aside. In a medium mixing bowl, whip the cream to soft or medium peaks (do not overbeat to stiff peaks).

Let the biscuits cool completely on the pan, then pull in half like hamburger buns. Top each biscuit bottom with a scoop of strawberries and their juices, a dollop of whipped cream, the biscuit top, more whipped cream, and more strawberries.

Make-ahead instructions
Make the biscuits days or weeks ahead and store tightly sealed in the freezer, then prep the rest of the components and assemble at the last minute.

Substitutions
Use store-bought canned biscuit dough to make this recipe super easy.

Other components you can use
Top these with any other stone fruit or berry, use cherry compote (page 259), or combine strawberry rhubarb compote (page 269) with fresh strawberries.

Pork chops with nectarine salsa

This is a recipe for delegating. And you're the one actually reading a headnote in a cookbook, so I'm assuming you're the boss! So you go ahead and make the salsa up to a day before serving, and then season the pork chops a few hours (or even a couple days) before grilling. Ask your partner or a friend to grill the pork chops, and direct them to arrange the chops on a plate and top with the salsa right before serving. After all, headnote-readers have bigger fish to fry (perhaps literally!).

———

To make the pork chops, sprinkle the chops with salt (use about ½ tsp per pound of pork, or 1 g per 140 g of pork) and pepper. Drizzle with the olive oil and coat evenly. Set aside in the fridge for at least 20 minutes (and up to a couple days).

Lightly oil the grill's grates and preheat to high when you're about ready to grill. Once hot, add the pork chops and grill until charred and cooked to 150°F [66°C] for medium, about 3 minutes per side.

Meanwhile, make the salsa. Place the tomato, jalapeño, and shallot in a mixing bowl. Lift the nectarines out of their juices and place in the mixing bowl. Add the cilantro, lime juice, and salt to the bowl and stir to combine.

Place the pork chops on a serving platter, top with the salsa, and serve.

⏱ 5+ MIN
◔ **15+ MIN**
ⓘ 30+ MIN

4 to 6 servings

For the pork chops:
8 boneless pork chops, ½ in [13 mm] thick
Salt
¼ tsp freshly ground black pepper
2 tsp extra-virgin olive oil, plus more for greasing the grill

For the nectarine salsa:
1 small or ½ large tomato, thinly sliced
1 jalapeño, thinly sliced (see recipe note)
1 shallot, thinly sliced
2 nectarines, sliced and macerated with 2 Tbsp sugar (see page 251)
2 Tbsp fresh cilantro
2 Tbsp lime juice
¼ tsp salt

Recipe note
I like to use the whole jalapeño here, since pork chops love heat. For a milder version, remove some of the pith and seeds before slicing.

Make-ahead instructions
The salsa can be made the day before serving. Assembled leftovers last for about a day.

Substitutions
For an even easier dinner, buy a really good pico de gallo and use that instead of the nectarine salsa. You can also use peaches or another stone fruit in this salsa.

Other components you can use
Caramelized tomatoes (page 101) are gorgeous as a topping for any grilled meat—use in place of the salsa with a handful of fresh basil leaves if you've got them around. Or drizzle with the cilantro lime dressing (page 147) or avocado tomatillo salsa verde (page 163) in place of the salsa.

Polish plum cake

I first had Polish plum cake in Melbourne, a city where you can find any Western or Eastern European pastry that your heart desires. While plums are traditional, you can absolutely experiment with other stone fruit or berries with this simple, accommodating batter. Just make sure your fruit isn't too ripe. It should yield a little to pressure, but shouldn't be too juicy.

⏱ 5+ MIN
◔ 15+ MIN
ⓘ **30+ MIN**

8 servings

For the cake:
10 or 11 halved small firm-ripe plums (365 g pitted), macerated with 3 Tbsp sugar (see page 251)
1½ cups [195 g] all-purpose flour
1½ tsp baking powder
¾ tsp salt
½ cup [100 g] granulated sugar
5 Tbsp [70 g] unsalted butter, at room temperature, plus more for greasing the pan
2 tsp lemon zest
1 tsp vanilla extract
2 large eggs
½ cup [120 g] buttermilk

For the topping:
2 Tbsp butter, cut into 12 pieces
2 Tbsp brown sugar
1 tsp ground cinnamon

To make the cake, set the macerated plums in a sieve over a bowl or the sink (discard the syrup). Preheat the oven to 350°F [180°C]. Butter a 9 in [23 cm] round cake pan and line it with a parchment round.

Sift together the flour, baking powder, and salt into a bowl. Set aside.

In the bowl of a stand mixer fitted with the paddle attachment, combine the granulated sugar, 5 Tbsp [70 g] of the butter, lemon zest, and vanilla. Beat for about 2 minutes on medium-high speed, until light and fluffy. Add the eggs one at a time with the mixer running on medium speed, letting each egg mix in completely before adding the next, and stopping to scrape down the sides once halfway through.

Add half the flour mixture, mix together, add all of the buttermilk, mix together, and add the rest of the flour mixture. Don't let the mixer run gratuitously, so as not to overmix, and stop as soon as there are no longer pockets of dry flour.

Transfer the batter to the prepared baking pan and spread it into an even layer. Arrange the plums cut-side up evenly over the surface. Press down lightly to embed them in the batter. To top the cake, dot the batter evenly with the butter pieces, and sprinkle with the brown sugar and cinnamon.

Bake for about 45 minutes, until a toothpick inserted in the center of the cake (between plums, not through a plum) comes out clean. Trace around the edge of the pan with a paring knife to loosen the cake, invert it onto a plate, and invert again. Let cool completely before slicing and serving.

Substitutions
You can use a similar amount of any other macerated stone fruit or berry here (see page 251). If you're using large plums or another large stone fruit, use only about 3, and quarter instead of halving them.

Cherry compote

Cherry compote has a texture like no other—unlike strawberries and raspberries, cherries have a tendency to hold together under pressure. Instead of falling apart, they stay more or less whole through the entire 20- to 25-minute simmer. This is best made in small batches, so make just what you need for each recipe in this section.

————

Makes about 1⅓ cups [350 g], enough to make any 1 recipe from this section

1 Tbsp water
4½ cups [575 g] pitted cherries
¼ cup [50 g] sugar

Place the water in a medium or large saucepan and add the cherries and sugar. Bring to a simmer over medium-high heat without stirring.

Once audibly simmering, give it a stir and let it gently boil uncovered for 20 to 25 minutes while stirring occasionally (gradually lower the heat so it doesn't rapidly boil). The cherries are done when their liquid has become syrupy and reduced down by about half (they will start out somewhat dry, but will give off a lot of liquid in the first 5 to 10 minutes).

Pour into a jar and cool to room temperature for about 30 minutes, then move to the fridge or freezer.

Recipe notes
You can use frozen cherries instead of fresh, especially if it's not summertime. Frozen cherries are less dense than fresh, so use 5¼ cups frozen (still 575 g). You can double this recipe, but be sure to use a wider pan (otherwise it will take much longer and your cherries will end up much softer).

Storage
Cherry compote freezes wonderfully for at least 3 months—store in containers small enough to use up at once after thawing. As long as you reduce it down sufficiently, it will keep in the fridge for about 1 week.

Store-bought alternatives
You can use cherry preserves for the Black Forest mousse (page 260) or cherry chèvre cheesecake recipes in this section. Keep in mind they will be a lot sweeter, so cut back as necessary.

Ways to use:
— For Black Forest mousse (page 260)
— Atop chèvre cheesecake (page 262)
— In cherry almond cheese babka (page 264)
— Use in place of the strawberry rhubarb compote in the Victoria sponge cake on page 272 (if you've got fresh cherries on hand, use them in place of the whole strawberries; otherwise just use the compote and whipped cream)
— Fold into whipped cream to make a fool (see page 270)
— Top the vegan double-chocolate orange tart (see page 240) with chilled cherry compote instead of orange supremes
— Top a bowl of oatmeal (see page 210)
— Fill a batch of choux buns (see page 214)
— Use in place of strawberries to make cherry shortcakes (see page 252)
— Warm or chilled, spoon over chocolate ice cream
— Serve with breakfast (for instance, pancakes, crêpes, waffles, or yogurt)
— Add a little balsamic vinegar to taste and serve with seared duck breast

Black Forest mousse

French chef and chemist Hervé This introduced the world to a chocolate mousse that's simultaneously very fine-dining and very semi-homemade. You just dilute dark chocolate with water, whip and chill it, and voilà! While you can definitely use an ice bath here, I never seem to have enough ice on hand. Instead, I like to dampen a tea towel, freeze it for a few minutes, and wrap it around the base of a steel stand mixer bowl. Counterintuitively, hot water freezes faster than cold, so don't use cold water in an attempt to freeze it more quickly.

⏱ **5+ MIN**
◔ 15+ MIN
◔ 30+ MIN

4 to 8 servings

7 oz [200 g] 70% dark chocolate
¾ cup [175 g] boiling water (see recipe notes)
1 batch cherry compote (page 259)

Drench two wet towels in some hot water from the tap, wring out slightly, then place in the freezer for about 10 minutes.

Place the dark chocolate in the stainless steel bowl of a stand mixer fitted with the whisk attachment. Top with the boiling water. Let it sit for 1 minute, then whisk on low speed to stir it together. Once it smooths out, wrap an ice-cold towel around the base of the stand mixer and increase the speed to medium-high. Beat for about 6 minutes, until it's thick and creamy. Replace the towel halfway through, once it loses its chill.

Spoon the mousse into small bowls or ramekins, chill, and serve topped with the cherry compote.

Recipe notes
Boil more water than is called for and measure just before using, as some of it will evaporate during boiling. Do not overbeat your chocolate or it will become gritty. If you do overbeat your chocolate, you can melt the whole thing down and start over.

Make-ahead instructions
Make 1 day ahead and refrigerate individual servings. Serve chilled.

Substitutions
Sprinkle on some cookie crumbs in addition to (or in place of) the fruit. You can also add a little dollop of whipped cream for a more authentically Black Forest flavor (or whipped coconut cream to keep it vegan).

Other components you can use
Top each ramekin of mousse with a dollop of strawberry rhubarb compote (page 269), macerated stone fruit or berries (page 251), or passion fruit curd (page 277) in place of the cherries.

Cherry chèvre cheesecake

In addition to being a goat cheese cake, this is also the G.O.A.T. cheesecake. You need to know 2 things to understand why it works: 1) Chèvre is basically just the goat version of cream cheese, and 2) goat cheese goes wonderfully with cherries.

———————

⏱ 5+ MIN
⊖ **15+ MIN**
ⓘ 30+ MIN

8 to 10 servings

23 [180 g] biscoff cookies
¼ cup [55 g] unsalted butter,
   melted, plus more for greasing
   the pan
Salt
8 oz [225 g] cream cheese,
   at room temperature
8 oz [225 g] fresh goat cheese,
   at room temperature
⅔ cup [130 g] sugar
2 large eggs
**1 cup [260 g] cherry compote,
   plus more for serving (page 259)**

Butter an 8 to 9 in [20 to 23 cm] cheesecake pan with a removable bottom, and preheat the oven to 350°F [180°C].

Place the cookies in a food processor fitted with the blade attachment. Pulse until finely ground. Add the melted butter and a pinch of salt and pulse several more times until it's the texture of wet sand.

Dump the cookie crumbs into the prepared cheesecake pan. Tamp down the crumbs into an even layer on the bottom. Bake for about 12 minutes, until it smells a little toasty and sets up. Set aside while you make the filling, and leave the oven on.

Wipe out the food processor so there aren't many crumbs. Add the cream cheese, goat cheese, sugar, eggs, and ¼ tsp salt. Blend together until smooth, but don't run it so long that it becomes fluffy. Pour the mixture over the baked crust and smooth out the top.

Bake the cheesecake for about 30 minutes. It's done once it's puffy around the edges but still a little jiggly when tapped on the counter. Let it cool at room temperature for about 30 minutes (it should quickly deflate). Then refrigerate until completely cool (about 3 hours in the fridge, but you can speed it up by freezing it for just 1 hour instead).

Once it's done chilling, trace a paring knife around the sides, remove the pan's collar by setting the pan on top of a big can of tomatoes, and then transfer to a serving plate. Top with the compote and serve with extra at the table.

Make-ahead instructions
This cheesecake is at its best after a full day of chilling, so try to make it the day before serving. Keep it covered and chilled in the refrigerator, then top with the compote right before serving. Leftover slices can be individually wrapped and then frozen for months.

Substitutions
You can use high-quality cherry preserves in place of the compote. If your preserves are very sweet, don't use a whole cup (but since you don't want it to look scant, serve with preserves at the table instead of topping the whole cake with them). You can also top the cheesecake super simply with fresh summer berries; place apricot jam in the microwave for just a few seconds to loosen it, and brush the berry topping with the jam.

Other components you can use
Top the cheesecake with a thin layer of strawberry rhubarb compote (about ½ cup [135 g], page 269), and then top with sliced strawberries. Or top it with strained macerated stone fruit or berries (page 251).

Cherry almond cheese babka

Babka would rather you didn't bog it down with lots of watery fruit. So while fresh cherries are delicious with cream cheese, it's hard to use enough of them to get a strong cherry flavor without making the dough soggy. Cherry compote (when reduced adequately) yields a babka that's packed with cherry flavor, without all the excess moisture that comes with fresh fruit. The other trick to ensuring a super flavorful loaf is rolling out your dough very thinly. If you don't, the filling layer will be thick and gloopy, and it will ooze out when you try to roll it up. With all that rolling and rising, this is a true weekend baking project, one that your Monday morning coworkers will be very thankful for.

⊘ 5+ MIN
⊖ 15+ MIN
ⓘ **30+ MIN**

2 loaves

For the dough:
¾ cup [180 g] milk
2 tsp active dry yeast
5 cups [650 g] all-purpose flour,
   plus more for dusting
½ cup [100 g] sugar
3 large eggs
1½ tsp salt
8 Tbsp [115 g] unsalted butter,
   at room temperature, plus
   more for greasing the pans

For the filling:
1 lb [455 g] cream cheese,
   at room temperature
1 large egg yolk
⅓ cup [65 g] sugar
¼ cup [35 g] all-purpose flour
1 tsp almond extract
**1 batch cherry compote
   (page 259), well-drained**

For the sugar glaze:
¼ cup [50 g] sugar
¼ cup [60 g] water

To make the dough, preheat the oven to 180°F [80°C], and then immediately turn it off and open the door a crack to cool down.

In the bowl of a stand mixer fitted with the dough hook, combine the milk and yeast. Stir together until the yeast dissolves. Add the flour, sugar, eggs, and salt and stir together on low speed, just until it forms a very shaggy dough, about 30 seconds. Add the butter to the dough 1 Tbsp at a time with the mixer running on low speed, waiting for each to be incorporated before adding the next one. Once all the butter has been added, scrape down the sides of the bowl, then increase the speed to medium. Knead for about 5 minutes, until it smooths out (if it sticks to the sides of the bowl, pause to scrape down the sides again. It will eventually start to pull away).

Remove the dough hook and cover the bowl with a plate. Place the bowl in the still moderately warm oven. Let the dough rise for 1 to 2 hours, just until it doubles in size.

Meanwhile, to make the filling, stir together the cream cheese, egg yolk, sugar, flour, and almond extract in a medium mixing bowl until completely combined. Use right away, or set it aside until the dough is ready.

Butter and line two 8 by 4 in [10 by 20 cm] loaf pans with parchment slings.

Once the babka dough has risen, transfer it to a countertop and divide it into two equal pieces. They should stick to the counter, but it should be easy to peel them away.   **cont'd**

Roll one of the dough pieces out to a very thin ⅛ in [3 mm] thick rectangle approximately 12 by 20 in [30 by 50 cm]. If it fights you, let it sit for about 5 minutes, then roll it out.

Spread half of the cream cheese mixture in a thin layer over the surface, leaving a 1 in [25 mm] border at one of the shorter sides and a ¼ in [6 mm] border everywhere else. Swirl half the cherry compote over the cream cheese mixture.

Roll up the dough, starting with the short side with the smaller border, all the way to the short side with the larger border. Pinch the ends together so the filling won't ooze out the sides, and then pinch the seam along the log gently to make sure it's well sealed. Lightly dust the outside all over with a little flour so that it's easier to move around. Repeat with the other half of the dough and filling.

Refrigerate both logs on a sheet pan for at least 45 minutes.

Use kitchen shears to cut each log in half lengthwise. Let them flop open cut-side up.

Criss-cross two halves at their centers so that their striped sides are both facing up in a big X. Continue criss-crossing them to twist together, being sure that their striped sides continue to face up the whole time. Once you get to the end, transfer the whole thing to a prepared loaf pan and scrunch it together so it's short enough to fit. Repeat with the other loaf, and place in the other loaf pan.

Cover both loaves loosely with plastic wrap and place them back in the slightly warm oven to rise for 60 to 75 minutes. Once they've risen to 1⅓ times their original size, remove from the oven and preheat the empty oven to 375°F [190°C].

Remove the plastic wrap and bake the loaves for about 70 minutes, just until their internal temperature reads about 200°F [93°C]. Loosely tent with foil about 45 minutes into baking. Remove from the pans to cool on a wire rack.

Meanwhile, to make the glaze, place the sugar in a small saucepan and add the water. Set over medium-high heat and bring to a simmer without stirring. Simmer for about 2½ minutes without stirring, until the sugar dissolves (don't continue simmering, or it'll turn into candy). Brush the warm glaze onto the babkas.

Recipe note
Do not store the glaze for longer than a couple hours, or it will crystalize. Don't sweat it if it crystalizes a tiny bit—it just needs to be brushable.

Make-ahead instructions
You can make the dough and filling the day before, then shape and bake the babkas the day you want to make them. Simply let the dough proof in the oven for the full amount of time, then punch it down, cover with plastic wrap, and place it in the fridge overnight.

Make the cream cheese filling, cover, and store in the fridge. Make and store the compote in the fridge as well. The next day, let the dough and filling sit at room temperature for about 30 minutes to warm up a little, and proceed with shaping the loaves.

Strawberry rhubarb compote

Strawberry and rhubarb are the reigning power couple of the late spring farmers' market. Individually, each has a lot going for it, but together they can do anything. Since it's a bit hard to find rhubarb out of season, I like to make a little extra compote to freeze for later in the year (see the note on store-bought alternatives to make any of the recipes in this section out of season).

————

Makes 1½ cups [400 g], enough to make either the chocolate rugelach or both the Victoria sponge cake and strawberry rhubarb fool

1 Tbsp water
2 cups [320 g] sliced strawberries
2 cups [300 g] sliced rhubarb
¼ cup plus 2 Tbsp [75 g] sugar
Pinch of salt

Place the water in a 10 in [25 cm] skillet, then add the strawberries, rhubarb, sugar, and salt. Bring to a simmer over medium heat without stirring.

Once it comes to a simmer, lower the heat to medium-low and give it a stir. Let it gently simmer, uncovered, for 40 to 45 minutes, stirring occasionally (do not intentionally mash up the pieces when you stir or it will take longer to reduce). You'll need to stir it more often during the last 10 minutes.

It's done once the whole thing has reduced by about half, and if you drag a spoon across the bottom it does not fill back in. Chill before serving.

Recipe note
If you halve this recipe, it will take more like 20 minutes to cook down completely in a 10 in [25 cm] skillet. To double it, it's best to use two separate pans, or it will take about 90 minutes to reduce. If you do decide to double it in one pot, only add 1 Tbsp of water (do not double the water), and use a taller, wider stockpot, because it will splatter more than a smaller batch.

Storage
When properly reduced to a paste, strawberry rhubarb compote keeps for up to 1 week in the refrigerator (discard if it starts to separate, gets moldy, or smells off), or for at least 3 months in the freezer with no loss of quality. Freeze in small containers, so that you can use a little at a time.

Store-bought alternatives
For many of the recipes in this section, you can absolutely use your favorite store-bought strawberry or raspberry jam or preserves instead of this compote.

Ways to use:
— Whipped into strawberry rhubarb fool (page 270)
— With Victoria sponge cake (page 272)
— In chocolate rugelach (page 274)
— On top of the chocolate mousse (see page 260)
— Use this compote and some sliced strawberries in place of the macerated fruit for the shortcakes on page 252
— Spread a thin layer on the cheesecake on page 262 and top with sliced strawberries
— Top a bowl of oatmeal (see page 210)
— Fill a batch of choux buns (see page 214)
— Spread on the cream scones on page 278
— Make a cheese board with Camembert or Brie, strawberry rhubarb compote, pecans, and a crusty, seedy whole-grain bread
— Make a PB&J with strawberry rhubarb compote in place of the jam
— Make a lemon poppy seed dressing, and use this jam instead of the honey or sweetener
— Swirl into plain yogurt

Strawberry rhubarb fool

A traditional English fool might be the absolute easiest thing you can make in this entire book. Literally whip some cream, fold in something soft and sweet, and there you have it! If you like a little crunch, you can also crumble on some cookies. But why complicate things?

———————

🕐 **5+ MIN**
◒ 15+ MIN
ⓘ 30+ MIN

4 to 6 servings

1½ cups [345 g] heavy whipping cream
2 Tbsp sugar
⅓ cup [90 g] chilled strawberry rhubarb compote (page 269), plus more for serving

In the bowl of a stand mixer fitted with the whisk attachment, combine the whipping cream and sugar. Beat on medium speed for about 3½ minutes, just until soft peaks form (do not overbeat, and keep a close eye on it). It should be dollopable, but not runny.

Drop 6 blobs of compote across the surface of the cream, and run a spatula through, cutting through each blob only once. Do not overmix. It should be extremely streaky.

Scoop into 4 to 6 serving dishes, top with a little more compote, and serve immediately.

Recipe note
If you don't have a stand mixer, whip the cream by hand. It doesn't take too long, and whipping by hand with a whisk makes it much harder to overbeat it.

Make-ahead instructions
Since pure whipped cream isn't stabilized in any way, a fool is best made at the last minute. But you can make the compote ahead, and place all the whipping cream ingredients in the bowl you plan to use, then cover and store that in the fridge so you can hit the ground running right after dinner.

Substitutions
Whip up some chilled coconut cream to make this vegan. Substitute store-bought strawberry preserves to make this super easy. For this recipe, try to find a strawberry preserve brand that is good quality and not too firmly set. Also try 1 cup [160 g] fresh summer berries halfmashed with the back of a fork.

Other components you can use
You can replace the strawberry rhubarb compote with ½ cup [130 g] cherry compote (page 259), ½ cup [130 g] passion fruit curd (page 277), or 1 cup [200 g] blood orange supremes (see page 235) tossed with a couple drops of vanilla bean paste.

Victoria sponge cake

⏱ 5+ MIN
◔ **15+ MIN**
ⓘ 30+ MIN

8 servings

For the cake:
1½ cups [195 g] all-purpose flour
1 cup [200 g] granulated sugar
1½ tsp baking powder
½ tsp salt
8 Tbsp [115 g] unsalted butter, at
   room temperature, plus more
   for greasing the pans
4 large eggs
½ cup [120 g] milk, at room
   temperature

For the whipped cream:
2 Tbsp cream cheese, chilled
   (optional)
2 tsp powdered sugar, plus more
   for dusting
½ cup [115 g] heavy whipping
   cream, cold

To assemble:
1 cup [140 g] sliced strawberries
**⅔ cup [175 g] strawberry rhubarb
   compote (page 269)**

To reverse-cream cake batter, you simply coat the flour in fat before introducing any liquid. If you've never tried it, you're in for a treat. By coating the flour in butter first, gluten doesn't form as easily as it would with a more traditional creaming method. This gets you an ultra-tender crumb. This is one of the easiest celebration cakes around, and comes together with just about 25 minutes of active time.

———

To make the cake, preheat the oven to 350°F [180°C]. Butter and line two 9 in [23 cm] cake pans with parchment rounds.

In the bowl of a stand mixer fitted with the paddle attachment, combine the flour, granulated sugar, baking powder, and salt on low speed just to combine. Add the butter and beat together until it looks like fine sand, 1½ to 2 minutes (start on low speed, then increase the speed to medium).

With the mixer running on medium speed, add 1 egg every 5 seconds or so, then drizzle in the milk. Be careful not to overmix—do not leave the mixer running while you're not adding anything.

Pour the batter into the prepared pans, dividing it equally into 2 thin layers. Spread the batter evenly.

Bake for about 17 minutes, until a toothpick inserted in the center comes out clean. Cool the cake layers on a wire rack.

To make the whipped cream, place the cream cheese, if using, and powdered sugar in the bowl of a stand mixer fitted with the whisk attachment. Beat for about 1 minute, scraping down the bowl once or twice, until it lightens and smooths out. If not using cream cheese, add the powdered sugar to the heavy cream and start here (see recipe note). Add the heavy cream, scrape the bottom of the bowl to loosen the cream cheese, and mix on medium speed for about 2½ minutes. As soon as it reaches medium-stiff peaks, stop whipping. Store in the fridge until you need it.

To assemble the cake, place one completely cooled cake layer on a plate or cake stand. Top with the whipped cream, spreading it out almost to the edges. Arrange the strawberries across the whipped cream, dollop the compote evenly across the surface, and spread it out over the strawberries. Top with the other cooled cake layer. Dust with powdered sugar and serve immediately, or refrigerate for a couple hours. Leftover slices should be stored in the fridge, and will keep for 1 to 2 days, but it's best served soon after assembling.

Recipe note
The cream cheese and powdered sugar in this recipe stabilizes the whipped cream and keeps it from becoming watery as it sits, but it's totally optional. It also adds a very subtle tangy flavor, which is lovely. If you omit it, add an additional 2 Tbsp of cream instead.

Make-ahead instructions
Prep all the components, bake the cake layers, and throw it all together at the last minute. The strawberries, whipped cream, and compote should be left in the fridge, and the cake should be left at room temperature (wrap it up after it cools).

Substitutions
You can use ½ cup [160 g] of store-bought strawberry preserves in place of the compote.

Other components you can use
Try the cherry compote on page 259 along with some pitted fresh cherries in place of the strawberries and compote. Or turn it into a very Australian sponge cake by replacing the fruit and compote with the passion fruit curd on page 277.

Chocolate rugelach

The best rugelach I've ever had was at Harold's Deli in northern New Jersey. Several pieces of rugelach adorned a single slab of cheesecake big enough to leave two to three adults rolling on the ground clutching their bellies. And while merely incidental, the rugelach were unmissable: crunchy on the outside, soft and flaky on the inside, and super flavorful. You'll find much the same here, with a tangy strawberry-rhubarb-chocolate filling.

———

⏱ 5+ MIN
◔ 15+ MIN
ⓘ **30+ MIN**

48 rugelach

For the dough:
2¼ cups [290 g] all-purpose flour, plus more for dusting
1 tsp salt
8 oz [225 g] cream cheese, cold
8 Tbsp [115 g] unsalted butter, cold
1 Tbsp plus 1 tsp apple cider vinegar

For the filling:
1½ cups [400 g] chilled strawberry rhubarb compote (page 269)
1 cup [150 g] finely chopped dark chocolate

For the egg wash:
1 large egg, beaten with 1 tsp water

To make the dough, place the flour in a food processor fitted with the blade attachment (if your food processor isn't large enough, work in two batches). Sprinkle evenly with the salt. Add the cream cheese and butter, cutting them into 2 Tbsp chunks as you add them.

Pulse the food processor a few times, stopping once the mixture looks crumbly and there are no giant pieces of butter or cream cheese. Sprinkle the apple cider vinegar evenly over the surface. Continue pulsing until the dough starts to clump.

Dump the dough onto a clean counter. Divide it into 4 blobs, and shape each blob into a disc. Wrap each disc in plastic wrap and place in the fridge for 2 hours (and up to 5 days).

Once the dough is chilled, preheat the oven to 350°F [180°C]. Line a few rimmed sheet pans with parchment paper.

Lightly flour a large cutting board. Roll one disc around in the flour, then use a rolling pin to roll it out very thinly into a circle about 14 in [35 cm] wide. Spread a little more than ⅓ cup [100 g] of compote into a thin layer, then sprinkle on about ¼ cup [35 g] of chocolate. Press the chocolate lightly into the compote with your fingertips. Slice into 12 wedges (slice pizza-style into quarters, then slice each quarter into thirds), and roll each wedge up from the wide end to the small pointed end.

Place the rugelach on a prepared sheet pan and brush with the egg wash. Bake for about 35 minutes, until the tops are golden brown and they've baked through. Slide the parchment onto the counter and let the rugelach cool completely. Repeat with the remaining batches.

Recipe note

If you do not roll your dough out enough, you will not be able to get many rolls out of each strip (they'll just look tri-folded), and your filing will ooze out the sides as you try to roll them up. Roll your dough out very thinly to prevent this.

Make-ahead instructions

Rugelach keep very well at room temperature for a day after baking, so feel free to bake them the day before you plan to serve them. To store longer, freeze them in an air-tight container for up to 3 months.

Substitutions

You can use seedless raspberry jam in place of the compote for a very similar flavor, or go further afield with another favorite. Cinnamon sugar with currants and chopped walnuts is a classic, but you could also use pretty much any fruit jam you'd like (apricot, guava, or quince are lovely—the more flavorful, the better).

Passion fruit curd

If you've got fresh passion fruit, all you need is a knife and a spoon to enjoy a delicious snack. But if you want to use that pulp in something, you're best off turning it into a curd, since passion fruit itself isn't particularly easy to cook or bake with. This curd recipe can be made with either fresh or frozen pulp, as long as it's 100% passion fruit. Make sure you leave those seeds in, as they add visual interest and a peppery crunch.

Makes about 3½ cups [920 g], enough to make all 3 recipes in this section

1½ cups [350 g] passion fruit pulp
6 large eggs
1 cup plus 2 Tbsp [225 g] sugar
¼ tsp salt
6 Tbsp [85 g] cold unsalted butter, cut into 4 pieces

Place the passion fruit pulp, eggs, sugar, and salt in a food processor fitted with the blade attachment. Pulse several times, stopping once it's completely combined.

Place the mixture in a small saucepan and set over medium-low heat. Whisk constantly until it thickens significantly. Gradually lower the heat and be careful not to let it overheat. It will start to thicken at around 140°F [60°C], and will fully thicken at around 167°F [75°C], which takes 10 to 15 minutes at medium-low. Don't go over 180°F [82°C].

Once the curd reaches the target temperature and consistency, remove from the heat and immediately add the butter, whisking constantly until it disappears completely.

Recipe note
If you don't have a food processor, you can whisk by hand, but you'll need to whisk the eggs and sugar together first until completely smooth, otherwise you'll end up with flecks of egg white in the finished product. Do not use a blender or you might pulverize the seeds. A food processor will just loosen the pulp while leaving the seeds whole.

Storage
Passion fruit curd will keep in the fridge for about 7 days, but it's best stored in the freezer for at least 3 months.

Store-bought alternatives
Any recipe in this section can be made with lemon curd (store-bought or homemade) instead of passion fruit curd. It'll obviously have a different flavor, but will still taste delicious.

Ways to use:
— Atop cream scones (page 278)
— In passion fruit olive oil cake (page 280)
— For frozen milk chocolate passion fruit bars (page 282)
— Give the Victoria sponge cake on page 272 an Australian vibe by replacing the compote with this curd

— Fold into whipped cream to make a passion fruit fool (see page 270)
— Replace the orange supremes on page 236 and top some ricotta with a dab of passion fruit curd, then sprinkle with pistachios or slivered almonds
— Top the mousse on page 260 with passion fruit curd instead of cherry compote
— Use in just about any recipe out there that calls for lemon curd
— Fill a layer cake (first pipe a dam of buttercream around the edge of one layer, fill with passion fruit curd, top with another layer, and frost it)

Cream scones with passion fruit curd

A scone is the best delivery device for passion fruit curd, and a cream scone is the easiest-ever kind to make. They require no kneading, no rolling out, no resting or laminating. But if you want to bring this recipe down to literally 1 minute of active time, just pop open and bake a can of buttermilk biscuits instead.

———

⏱ **5+ MIN**
◐ 15+ MIN
ⓘ 30+ MIN

10 to 12 scones

2½ cups [325 g] all-purpose flour
⅓ cup [65 g] sugar
¼ cup [55 g] cold unsalted butter, cut into chunks
1 Tbsp baking powder
1 tsp salt
1⅓ cups [315 g] heavy whipping cream, plus more for brushing
Passion fruit curd (page 277), for serving

Preheat the oven to 425°F [220°C] and line a sheet pan with parchment paper.

Place the flour, sugar, butter, baking powder, and salt in a mixing bowl. Use the tips of your fingers to work the butter into the flour until there are no pieces bigger than small peas. Add the whipping cream and stir together (do not overmix).

Use 2 spoons to drop 10 to 12 craggy blobs of dough onto the prepared sheet pan, brush with more cream, and bake for 15 minutes until puffy and golden brown. Cool on the parchment paper and enjoy warm or at room temperature with about 1 Tbsp of passion fruit curd per scone.

Other components you can use
Cream scones also go nicely with strawberry rhubarb compote (page 269).

Passion fruit olive oil cake

This recipe is inspired by chef and cookbook author Lucy Cufflin's lemon curd cake, with its charmingly wonky swirls of curd in a sea of butter cake. This one marries olive oil and passion fruit instead, with its own lopsided charm.

⸻

⏱ 5+ MIN
◐ 15+ MIN
ⓘ 30+ MIN

8 servings

¾ cup [150 g] sugar
½ cup [105 g] extra-virgin olive oil, plus more for greasing the pan
3 large eggs
⅔ cup [175 g] passion fruit curd (page 277) for the batter, plus ⅔ cup [175 g] for the swirls
1⅓ cups [175 g] all-purpose flour
1¼ tsp salt
1 tsp baking powder

Preheat the oven to 375°F [190°C]. Oil a 9 in [23 cm] cake pan and line the bottom with a parchment round.

Place the sugar, olive oil, eggs, and ⅔ cup [175 g] of the passion fruit curd in a mixing bowl. Stir together until completely homogenous.

Sift the flour, salt, and baking powder into the wet ingredients. Stir just until combined (do not overmix).

Scrape the batter into the prepared cake pan, smooth it out, and then top it evenly with spoonfuls of the remaining ⅔ cup [175 g] passion fruit curd. You should end up with about 12 spoonfuls spaced across the surface. Drag the back of your spoon through the cake in figure-eights so that you catch each blob once or twice. You should end up with thin swirls across the surface (don't overswirl, or it will affect the texture of the cake).

Bake for about 30 minutes, until a toothpick inserted into the center of the cake (avoiding the passion fruit) comes out clean. Let it sit for about 3 minutes in the pan, then trace around the edge with a knife, invert the cake onto a parchment-covered plate, peel off the parchment from the bottom, and invert again onto a wire rack. Peel the parchment off the top and let the cake cool before slicing.

Substitutions
Use store-bought lemon curd in place of passion fruit curd.

Frozen milk chocolate passion fruit bars

This recipe started out as a regular-old chocolate passion fruit slice. But when I was in a hurry one day, I threw them in the freezer, and I never looked back.

⊘ 5+ MIN
⊖ 15+ MIN
ⓘ **30+ MIN**

16 servings

For the shortbread crust:
11 Tbsp [155 g] unsalted butter, at room temperature, plus more for greasing the pan
½ cup [55 g] powdered sugar
1½ cups [195 g] all-purpose flour
¼ tsp salt

For the milk chocolate ganache:
½ cup [115 g] heavy whipping cream
10 oz [285 g] chopped milk chocolate
1⅓ cups [350 g] passion fruit curd (page 277)

To make the shortbread crust, butter an 8 by 8 in [20 by 20 cm] pan and line it with a parchment sling.

Place the butter in the bowl of a stand mixer fitted with the paddle attachment. Beat on medium-high speed for about 30 seconds, just to lighten it slightly. Add the powdered sugar, mix on low speed until incorporated, and then continue to beat on medium-high speed until it's light and fluffy, about 1 minute. Add the flour and salt and mix together on low speed until it forms small clumps. Scrape down the sides and beaters, then mix on medium speed until it forms large clumps.

Dump the dough into the prepared pan. Use an offset spatula to spread the dough into an even layer across the bottom, then pat it down with your fingers until uniform. If it becomes too sticky, pop it in the freezer for a couple minutes. Dock the dough with a fork. Place the unbaked shell in the freezer until completely solid, about 20 minutes. Meanwhile, preheat the oven to 400°F [205°C].

Bake the shell until light golden brown, about 17 minutes. Cool on a wire rack in the pan.

To make the milk chocolate ganache, heat the cream in the microwave (or on the stove over medium heat) just until simmering. Remove from the heat, add the chocolate, and let it sit for a minute. Whisk together until it's completely smooth. Do not reheat—either pour it or spread it immediately.

Pour or spread the ganache on the shortbread and smooth into an even layer. Refrigerate for at least 1 hour, until completely set.

Spread the curd into a single layer over the ganache. Loosely cover the pan and freeze until completely set (about 2 hours). Trace around the parchment-free edge with a butter knife, lift the parchment sling out of the pan, and slice the shortbread into 16 bars while frozen. Wipe the blade between each slice for clean slices. Place slices in an airtight container, and freeze for up to 3 months.

Acknowledgments

Thanks to everyone who made this book better, handier, and realer than it ever could've been otherwise. Thanks to Andrianna Yeatts, Sarah Billingsley, Lizzie Vaughan, Claire Gilhuly, Margo Winton Parodi, Jessica Ling, Erin Slonaker, Cecilia Santini, Gabby Vanacore, and everyone at Chronicle who had a hand in this project.

Thanks to Simon for giving *Piecemeal* its name, for thinking the idea through with me while we hiked, for suggesting that maybe the components shouldn't all be vegetables, and for your patience with me when I scoffed at you and insisted you were obviously wrong. I can always count on you to be fully Simon, never anything less, and I'm lucky for that.

Thanks to my family for lending me your kitchens while I was traveling around the US and doing some preliminary recipe developing for this book, for only occasionally rolling your eyes when I went on about oven calibration and thermometers, and for taste-testing everything with me. My last book, *A Dish for All Seasons*, was produced during the near-two-year Australian border closure and 8½ months of strict Melbourne lockdowns. I'm fortunate to have gotten to experience this book's process while safely in the company of friends and family.

Index